THE AUTHOR: Takuan Sōhō (1573–1645) was a prelate of the Rinzai Sect of Zen, well remembered for his strength of character and acerbic wit; and he was also gardener, poet, tea master, prolific author and a pivotal figure in Zen painting and calligraphy. His religious training began at the age of ten. He entered the Rinzai sect at the age of fourteen and was appointed abbot of the Daitokuji, a major Zen temple in Kyoto, at the age of thirty-five. After a disagreement on ecclesiastical appointments with the second Tokugawa shogun, he was banished in 1629 to a far northern province. Coming under a general amnesty on the death of the shogun, he returned to society three years later to be, among other things, a confidant of the third Tokugawa shogun.

THE TRANSLATOR: William Scott Wilson took his B.A. at Dartmouth College, graduated as a Japanese specialist from the Monterey Institute of Foreign Studies, and received his M.A. in Japanese literature from the University of Washington. He became acquainted with Japan at first-hand in 1966 on a coastal expedition—by kayak—from the western Japanese port of Sasebo to Tokyo. He later lived in the potter's village of Bizen, studied as a special student at Aichi Prefectural University, and was a counselor at the Japanese Consulate-General in Seattle. He now lives in his native Florida.

Among his highly regarded translations of original works of literature are *Hagakure: The Book of the Samurai* and *The Roots of Wisdom: Saikontan*.

The
Unfettered
Mind

Writings of the Zen Master
to the Sword Master

Takuan Sōhō
translated by William Scott Wilson

KODANSHA INTERNATIONAL
Tokyo・New York・London

Distributed in the United States by Kodansha America, Inc., 114 Fifth Avenue, New York, N.Y. 10011, and in the United Kingdom and continental Europe by Kodansha Europe Ltd., Gillingham House, 38-44 Gillingham Street, London SW1V 1HU. Published by Kodansha International Ltd., 17-14 Otowa 1-chome, Bunkyo-ku, Tokyo 112, and Kodansha America, Inc.
LC 86-45072
ISBN 0-87011-851-X
ISBN 4-7700-1351-5 (in Japan)
First edition, 1986
First paperback edition, 1987
93 10 9 8 7 6

Dedicated to
Gary Miller Haskins

CONTENTS

Foreword

The sword, which we in the West are encouraged to beat into plowshares, and the correct techniques and mentality for using it are the main topics of the three essays presented here. The essays, two of which were letters to master swordsmen, were written by a Zen monk, Takuan Sōhō, whose vow was the enlightenment and salvation of all sentient beings. What business a priest of Buddhism had with an instrument of destruction and advice on how to become more proficient with it is unlikely to be immediately clear to the Western reader.

The sword and the spirit have long been closely associated by the Japanese. In both history and mythology, the sword figures as an instrument of life and death, of purity and honor, of authority and even of divinity. Historically, it was possession of the iron sword that helped secure the islands for the migrants from the Asian mainland in the second and third centuries A.D., the success of that conquest raising the sword to an object of ceremony as well as one of victory. Mythologically, it was the sword found within the Yamata no Orochi, a dragonlike serpent killed by the god of storms, that was to become one of the Three Imperial Regalia, symbols of power and purity revered by the Japanese for nearly two millenia. Practically, it has been the samurai class with the sword on one side and the spiritual on the other, that has been the inspiration for many of the country's lasting values.

This association was not dimmed by the conversion of the samurai to other occupations a little over a century ago. Even today, the infrequent forging of a new Japanese sword takes place in a highly spiritual atmosphere. The work itself is preceded by prayers to the proper divinities and the performance of purification rites, and is executed while wearing ceremonial robes without and maintaining a reverential frame of mind within. The owner of the sword is expected to respond to his good fortune in a like mentality; and, indeed, when the Japanese businessman finds a quiet moment at home to unwrap, unsheathe, and lightly powder his sword against rust, it is considered to be an exercise in meditation, not the idle admiration of a work of art.

The sword, the spiritual exercise and the unfettered mind are the pivots upon which these essays turn. With effort and patience, the writer reminds us, they should become one. We are to practice, practice with whatever we may have at hand, until the enemies of our own anger, hesitation and greed are cut down with the celerity and decisiveness of the stroke of a sword.

There are several editions of the works included here, but they seem to be without significant differences. I have based these translations on the texts given in *Nihon no Zen Goroku, Vol. 13*, which in turn uses those found in *Takuan Oshō Zenshū*, published by the Takuan Oshō Zenshu Kanko Kai.

In appreciation I would like to sincerely thank Ms. Agnes Youngblood, who helped me through parts of the translation where I had the most difficulty; John Siscoe for his encouragement and suggestions; and Prof. Jay Rubin and Teruko Chin of the University of Washington for helping me with background material over a distance of four thousand miles and a few inches of snow. Any and all mistakes are my own.

Introduction

Takuan Sōhō was Zen monk, calligrapher, painter, poet, gardener, tea master, and, perhaps, inventor of the pickle that even today retains his name. His writings were prodigious (the collected works fill six volumes), and are a source of guidance and inspiration to the Japanese people today, as they have been for three and a half centuries. Adviser and confidant to high and low, he seems to have moved freely through almost every stratum of society, instructing both shogun and emperor and, as legend has it, being friend and teacher to the swordsman/artist, Miyamoto Musashi. He seems to have remained unaffected by his fame and popularity, and at the approach of death he instructed his disciples, "Bury my body in the mountain behind the temple, cover it with dirt and go home. Read no sutras, hold no ceremony. Receive no gifts from either monk or laity. Let the monks wear their robes, eat their meals, and carry on as on normal days." At his final moment, he wrote the Chinese character for *yume* ("dream"), put down the brush, and died.

Takuan was born in 1573 in the village of Izushi in the province of Tajima, an area of deep snows and mountain mists. Izushi is a village ancient enough to be mentioned in both of the early histories of Japan, the *Kojiki* (A.D. 712) and the *Nihon-gi* (A.D. 720), and the countryside around it is sprinkled with relics of earlier ages, as well as ancient burial mounds and pottery shards of extreme antiquity. Although born into a samurai family of the Miura clan at the culmination of 150 years of civil strife, Takuan entered a monastery at the age of ten to study the Jōdo sect of Buddhism, moving on to practice the Rinzai sect of Zen at the age of fourteen and becoming the abbot of the Daitokuji, a major Zen temple in Kyoto, at the unprecedented age of thirty-five.

In 1629, Takuan became involved in what was referred to as the "Purple Robe Affair," in which he opposed the shogunate's decision to cancel the emperor's power to make appointments to high ecclesiastical ranks and offices. For his opposition, he was banished to what is now Yamagata Prefecture, and it was in this far northern hinterland where the first and the last of the three essays in this volume were written. He was included in the general amnesty upon the shogun's death, and returned to Kyoto in 1632. During the following years he befriended and taught Zen to the abdicated but very influential emperor, Go-Mizunoo, and so impressed the new shogun, Tokugawa Iemitsu, who constantly sought his friendship, that he founded the Tōkaiji in 1638 at the shogun's behest. And, while friendly to both shogun and emperor, he adamantly steered clear of the political quarrels that so often embroiled the shogunate and the chrysanthemum throne.

To the end, Takuan is said to have followed his own independent, eccentric and sometimes bitter way. His strength and angularity are apparent in his calligraphy and painting as well as in the following essays, and it is interesting that we can, perhaps, have a taste of the man's character by simply

13

sampling a dish of *takuanzuke*, a pickle made from the giant Japanese radish.

His life may be summed up by his own admonition, "If you follow the present-day world, you will turn your back on the Way; if you would not turn your back on the Way, do not follow the world."

It is said that Takuan sought to infuse the spirit of Zen into every aspect of life that caught his interest, such things as calligraphy, poetry, gardening and the arts in general. This he also did with the art of the sword. Living during the last days of the violent feudal strife which culminated, essentially, with the Battle of Sekigahara in 1600, Takuan was acquainted not only with the peace and sublimity of the artist and tea master, but also with the confrontation—victory and defeat—of the warrior and general. Among the latter were such disparate figures as Ishida Mitsunari, a powerful general who supported Toyotomi Hideyoshi; Kuroda Nagamasa, a Christian daimyo who engineered Mitsunari's downfall; and, especially, his friend Yagyū Munenori, head of the Yagyū Shinkage school of swordsmanship and teacher to two generations of shoguns. To these men and these times, Takuan addressed himself no less than to others.

Of the three essays included in this translation, two were letters: *Fudōchishinmyōroku*, "The Mysterious Record of Immovable Wisdom," written to Yagyū Munenori; and *Taiaki*, "Annals of the Sword Taia," written perhaps to Munenori or possibly to Ono Tadaaki, head of the Ittō school of swordsmanship and also an official instructor to the shogun's family and close retainers. The circumstances of how they came to be written are unclear, although the frank advice and rather Confucian admonishment to Munenori at the end of *Fudōchi-*

14

shinmyōroku adds another interesting if somewhat puzzling dimension to this work.

As a whole, all three are addressed to the samurai class, and all three seek to unify the spirit of Zen with the spirit of the sword. The advice given is a blend of the practical, technical and philosophical aspects of confrontation. Individually and broadly speaking, one could say that *Fudō-chishinmyōroku* deals not only with technique, but with how the self is related to the Self during confrontation and how an individual may become a unified whole. *Taiaki*, on the other hand, deals more with the psychological aspects of the relationship between the self and the other. Between these, *Reirōshū*, "The Clear Sound of Jewels," deals with the fundamental nature of the human being, with how a swordsman, daimyo—or any person, for that matter—can know the difference between what is right and what is mere selfishness, and can understand the basic question of knowing when and how to die.

All three essays turn the individual to knowledge of himself, and hence to the art of life.

Swordsmanship as an expression of technique alone and meditative Zen had long existed in Japan, Zen having become firmly established around the end of the twelfth century. With Takuan they achieved a true coalescence, and his writings and opinions on the sword have been extraordinarily influential in the direction the art of Japanese swordsmanship has taken from that day to the present, for it is an art still fervently practiced, and it reflects a significant spectrum of the Japanese outlook on life. Firmly establishing the unity of Zen and the sword, they have influenced the writings of the great masters of the time and produced a spinoff of documents which con-

15

tinue to be read and applied, such as the *Heihō Kadensho* of Yagyū Munenori and the *Gorin no Sho* of Miyamoto Musashi. The styles of these men differed, but their conclusions weave together a lofty level of insight and understanding, whether it be expressed as the "freedom and spontaneity" of Musashi, the "ordinary mind that knows no rules" of Munenori or the "unfettered mind" of Takuan.

For Takuan, the culmination was not one of death and destruction, but rather of enlightenment and salvation. Confrontation, in the "right" mind, would not only give life, but give it more abundantly.

The Mysterious
Record of
Immovable Wisdom

The term *ignorance* means the absence of enlightenment. Which is to say, delusion.

Abiding place means the place where the mind stops.

In the practice of Buddhism, there are said to be fifty-two stages, and within these fifty-two, the place where the mind stops at one thing is called the *abiding place*. Abiding signifies stopping, and *stopping* means the mind is being detained by some matter, which may be any matter at all.

To speak in terms of your own martial art, when you first notice the sword that is moving to strike you, if you think of meeting that sword just as it is, your mind will stop at the sword in just that position, your own movements will be undone, and you will be cut down by your opponent. This is what *stopping* means.

Although you see the sword that moves to strike you, if your mind is not detained by it and you meet the rhythm of the advancing sword; if you do not think of striking your opponent and no thoughts or judgments remain; if the instant you see the swinging sword your mind is not the least bit detained and you move straight in and wrench the sword away from him; the sword that was going to cut you down will become your own, and, contrarily, will be the sword that cuts down your opponent.

In Zen this is called "Grabbing the spear and, contrariwise, piercing the man who had come to pierce you." The spear is a weapon. The heart of this is that the sword you wrest from your adversary becomes the sword that cuts him down. This is what you, in your style, call "No-Sword."

Whether by the strike of the enemy or your own thrust,

19

whether by the man who strikes or the sword that strikes, whether by position or rhythm, if your mind is diverted in any way, your actions will falter, and this can mean that you will be cut down.

If you place yourself before your opponent, your mind will be taken by him. You should not place your mind within yourself. Bracing the mind in the body is something done only at the inception of training, when one is a beginner.

The mind can be taken by the sword. If you put your mind in the rhythm of the contest, your mind can be taken by that as well. If you place your mind in your own sword, your mind can be taken by your own sword. Your mind stopping at any of these places, you become an empty shell. You surely recall such situations yourself. They can be said to apply to Buddhism.

In Buddhism, we call this stopping of the mind *delusion*. Thus we say, "The affliction of abiding in ignorance."

THE IMMOVABLE WISDOM OF ALL BUDDHAS

Immovable means unmoving.

Wisdom means the wisdom of intelligence.

Although wisdom is called immovable, this does not signify any insentient thing, like wood or stone. It moves as the mind is wont to move: forward or back, to the left, to the right, in the ten directions and to the eight points; and the mind that does not stop at all is called *immovable wisdom*.

Fudō Myōō grasps a sword in his right hand and holds a rope in his left hand.[1] He bares his teeth and his eyes flash with anger. His form stands firmly, ready to defeat the evil spirits that would obstruct the Buddhist Law. This is not hidden in any country anywhere. His form is made in the shape of a protector of Buddhism, while his embodiment is that of immovable wisdom. This is what is shown to living things.

Seeing this form, the ordinary man becomes afraid and has no thoughts of becoming an enemy of Buddhism. The man who is close to enlightenment understands that this manifests immovable wisdom and clears away all delusion. For the man who can make his immovable wisdom apparent and who is able to physically practice this mental dharma as well as Fudō Myōō, the evil spirits will no longer proliferate. This is the purpose of Fudō Myōō's tidings.

What is called Fudō Myōō is said to be one's unmoving mind and an unvacillating body. *Unvacillating* means not being detained by anything.

Glancing at something and not stopping the mind is called *immovable*. This is because when the mind stops at something, as the breast is filled with various judgments, there are various movements within it. When its movements cease, the stopping mind moves, but does not move at all.

If ten men, each with a sword, come at you with swords slashing, if you parry each sword without stopping the mind at each action, and go from one to the next, you will not be lacking in a proper action for every one of the ten.

Although the mind act ten times against ten men, if it does not halt at even one of them and you react to one after another, will proper action be lacking?

But if the mind stops before one of these men, though you parry his striking sword, when the next man comes, the right action will have slipped away.

Considering that the Thousand-Armed Kannon has one thousand arms on its one body, if the mind stops at the one holding a bow, the other nine hundred and ninety-nine will be useless.[2] It is because the mind is not detained at one place that all the arms are useful.

As for Kannon, to what purpose would it have a thousand arms attached to one body? This form is made with the intent of pointing out to men that if their immovable wisdom is let go, even if a body have a thousand arms, every one will be of use.

When facing a single tree, if you look at a single one of its red leaves, you will not see all the others. When the eye is not set on any one leaf, and you face the tree with nothing at all in mind, any number of leaves are visible to the eye without limit. But if a single leaf holds the eye, it will be as if the remaining leaves were not there.

One who has understood this is no different from the Kannon with a thousand arms and a thousand eyes.

The ordinary man simply believes that it is blessed because of its thousand arms and its thousand eyes. The man of half-baked wisdom, wondering how anybody could have a thousand eyes, calls it a lie and gives in to slander. But if now one understands a little better, he will have a respectful belief based on principle and will not need the simple faith of the ordinary man or the slander of the other, and he will understand that Buddhism, with this one thing, manifests its principle well.

All religions are like this. I have seen that Shinto especially is like this.

The ordinary man thinks only on the surface. The man who attacks Buddhism is even worse.

This religion, that religion, there are various kinds but at their deepest points they are all settled in one conclusion.

At any rate, when one practices discipline and moves from the beginner's territory to immovable wisdom, he makes a return and falls back to the level of the beginning, the abiding place.

There is a reason for this.

Again, we can speak with reference to your own martial art. As the beginner knows nothing about either his body posture or the positioning of his sword, neither does his mind stop anywhere within him. If a man strikes at him with the sword, he simply meets the attack without anything in mind.

As he studies various things and is taught the diverse ways of how to take a stance, the manner of grasping his sword and where to put his mind, his mind stops in many places. Now if he wants to strike at an opponent, he is extraordinarily discomforted. Later, as days pass and time piles up, in accordance with his practice, neither the postures of his body nor the ways of grasping the sword are weighed in his mind. His mind simply becomes as it was in the beginning when he knew nothing and had yet to be taught anything at all.

In this one sees the sense of the beginning being the same as the end, as when one counts from one to ten, and the first and last numbers become adjacent.

In other things—musical pitch, for example, when one moves from the beginning lowest pitch to the final highest pitch—the lowest and the highest become adjacent.[3]

We say that the highest and the lowest come to resemble each other. Buddhism, when you reach its very depths, is like the man who knows nothing of either the Buddha or the Buddhist Law. It has neither adornment nor anything else that would draw men's attention to it.

The ignorance and afflictions of the beginning, abiding place and the immovable wisdom that comes later become one. The function of the intellect disappears, and one ends in a state of No-Mind-No-Thought. If one reaches the deepest point, arms, legs and body remember what to do, but the mind does not enter into this at all.

The Buddhist priest Bukkoku wrote:[4]

> Although it does not
>   mindfully keep guard,
> In the small mountain fields
>   the scarecrow
>   does not stand in vain.

Everything is like this.

To make a scarecrow for the mountain fields, one fashions a human figure and puts in its hands a bow and arrow. The birds and beasts see this and flee. Although this figure has absolutely no mind, if the deer become frightened and run away, insofar as it has fulfilled its function, it has not been created in vain.

This is an example of the behavior of the people who have reached the depths of any Way. While hands, feet and body may move, the mind does not stop anyplace at all, and one does not know where it is. Being in a state of No-Thought-No-Mind, one has come to the level of the scarecrow of the mountain fields.

Of the common man who has not found his path, we can say that from the very beginning he has had no wisdom and it will never come forth, whatever the circumstances. The wisdom that is highest of all, being in the most remote of all places, will absolutely not come forth. Finally, the half-baked know-it-all lets his wisdom come right off the top of his head, and this is ridiculous. The decorum of the priests of today can surely be thought of in such a light. This is a matter of shame.

There is such a thing as training in principle, and such a thing as training in technique.

Principle is as I have already explained above: when you arrive, nothing is noticed. It is simply as though you had discarded all concentration. I have written at length about this above.

If you do not train in technique, but only fill your breast with principle, your body and your hands will not function. Training in technique, if put into terms of your own martial art, is in the training that if practiced over and over again makes the five body postures one.

Even though you know principle, you must make yourself perfectly free in the use of technique. And even though you may wield the sword that you carry with you well, if you are unclear on the deepest aspects of principle, you will likely fall short of proficiency

Technique and principle are just like the two wheels of a cart.

THE INTERVAL INTO WHICH NOT EVEN A HAIR CAN BE ENTERED

There is such a thing as an interval into which not even a hair can be put. We can speak about this in terms of your own martial art.

"Interval" is when two things come one upon another, and not even a hairsbreadth can be slipped in between them.

When you clap your hands and, just at that instant, let out a yell, the interval between clapping your hands and letting out a yell will not allow the entrance of a hairsbreadth.

This is not a matter of clapping your hands, thinking about yelling, and then doing so, which would result in there being an interval in between. You clap your hands and, just at that instant, let out a sound.

In just the same way, if the mind stops with the sword with which a man is going to strike you, there will be an interval, and your own action will be lost. But if in the interval between your opponent's striking sword and your own action you cannot introduce even the breadth of a hair, your opponent's sword should become your own.

In Zen discussions we have the same thing. In Buddhism we abhor this stopping and the mind remaining with one thing or another. We call this stopping *affliction*.

It is like a ball riding a swift-moving current: we respect the mind that flows on like this and does not stop for an instant in any place.

THE ACTION OF SPARK AND STONE

There is such a thing as the action of spark and stone. This is the same as the foregoing. No sooner have you struck the stone than the light appears. Since the light appears just as you strike the stone, there is neither interval nor interstice. This also signifies the absence of the interval that would stop the mind.

It would be a mistake to understand this simply as celerity. Rather, it underscores the point that the mind should not be detained by things; it says that even with speed it is essential that the mind does not stop. When the mind stops, it will be grasped by the opponent. On the other hand, if the mind contemplates being fast and goes into quick action, it will be captured by its own contemplation.

Among the poems of Saigyō is the following:

> One hears of you solely
>   as a man who abhors the world.
> I can only hope
>   your mind be not detained
>   by this transient lodging.

He attributes this poem to the courtesan of Eguchi.[5]

If you took the latter part of this verse, "I can only hope / your mind be not detained . . ." it could be cited as hitting the very essence of the martial arts. It is essential that the mind not be detained.

In Zen, if asked, "What is the Buddha?" one should raise a clenched fist. If asked, "What is the ultimate meaning of the Buddhist Law?" before the words have died away, one should respond, "A single branch of the flowering plum" or "The cypress in the garden."

It is not a matter of selecting an answer either good or bad. We respect the mind that does not stop. The non-stopping mind is moved by neither color nor smell.

Although the form of this unmoving mind is revered as a god, respected as a Buddha, and called the Mind of Zen or the Ultimate Meaning, if one thinks things through and afterwards speaks, even though he utter golden words and mysterious verses, it will be merely the affliction of the abiding place.

Can it not be said that the action of stone and spark has the speed of a lightning flash?

It is immovable wisdom when one is called and answers

27

"Yes?" immediately. When one is called, to hesitate over the why and wherefore of the request is the affliction of the abiding place.

The mind that stops or is moved by something and sent into confusion—this is the affliction of the abiding place, and this is the common man. To be called, to respond without interval, is the wisdom of all Buddhas.

The Buddha and all sentient beings are not two. Such a mind is called a god or a Buddha.

Although there are many Ways—the Way of the Gods, the Way of Poetry, the Way of Confucius—they all share the clarity of this one mind.

When explaining the mind with words, we say such things as "All people possess this mind" or "Good and bad events morning and evening are according to Karma" or "Whether one leaves his house or brings his country to ruin is a reflection of one's character, for both good and evil depend on one's mind." If people are to know what this mind is like, they will only be confused by it if there is no truly enlightened person to show them.

In this world, there are surely people who do not know the mind. It is also clear that people exist who do understand, rare as this may be. Although there occasionally are people who do understand, it does not often happen that they act accordingly; then, although they explain the mind well, it is doubtful that they understand it in depth.

One may explain water, but the mouth will not become wet. One may expound fully on the nature of fire, but the mouth will not become hot.

Without touching real water and real fire, one will not know these things. Even explaining a book will not make it under-

28

stood. Food may be concisely defined, but that alone will not relieve one's hunger.

One is not likely to achieve understanding from the explanation of another.

In this world, there are Buddhists and there are Confucianists who explain the mind, but their actions are not like their explanations. The minds of such people are not truly enlightened. If people are not thoroughly enlightened about their own particular minds, they will have no understanding.

Many who study do not understand the mind, but it is not a matter of numbers. There is not one of them with a good frame of mind. It must be said that the enlightening of one's mind depends on the depths of one's efforts.

WHERE ONE PUTS THE MIND

We say that:

If one puts his mind in the action of his opponent's body, his mind will be taken by the action of his opponent's body.[6]

If he puts his mind in his opponent's sword, his mind will be taken by that sword.

If he puts his mind in thoughts of his opponent's intention to strike him, his mind will be taken by thoughts of his opponent's intention to strike him.

If he puts his mind in his own sword, his mind will be taken by his own sword.

If he puts his mind in his own intention of not being struck, his mind will be taken by his intention of not being struck.

If he puts his mind in the other man's stance, his mind will be taken by the other man's stance.

What this means is that there is no place to put the mind.

A certain person once said, "No matter where I put my mind, my intentions are held in check in the place where my mind goes, and I lose to my opponent. Because of that, I place my mind just below my navel and do not let it wander.[7] Thus am I able to change according to the actions of my opponent."

This is reasonable. But viewed from the highest standpoint of Buddhism, putting the mind just below the navel and not allowing it to wander is a low level of understanding, not a high one. It is at the level of discipline and training. It is at the level of seriousness. Or of Mencius' saying, "Seek after the lost mind."[8] This is not the highest level either. It has the sense of seriousness. As for the "lost mind," I have written about this elsewhere, and you can take a look at it there.

If you consider putting your mind below your navel and not letting it wander, your mind will be taken by the mind that thinks of this plan. You will have no ability to move ahead and will be exceptionally unfree.

This leads to the next question, "If putting my mind below my navel leaves me unable to function and without freedom, it is of no use. In what part of my body, then, should I put my mind?"

I answered, "If you put it in your right hand, it will be taken by the right hand and your body will lack its functioning. If you put your mind in the eye, it will be taken by the eye, and your body will lack its functioning. If you put your mind in your right foot, your mind will be taken by the right foot, and your body will lack its functioning.

"No matter where you put it, if you put the mind in one place, the rest of your body will lack its functioning."

"Well, then, where does one put his mind?"

I answered, "If you don't put it anywhere, it will go to all parts of your body and extend throughout its entirety. In this way, when it enters your hand, it will realize the hand's function. When it enters your foot, it will realize the foot's function. When it enters your eye, it will realize the eye's function.

"If you should decide on one place and put the mind there, it will be taken by that place and lose its function. If one thinks, he will be taken by his thoughts.

"Because this is so, leave aside thoughts and discrimination, throw the mind away from the entire body, do not stop it here and there, and when it does visit these various places, it will realize function and act without error."

Putting the mind in one place is called *falling into one-sidedness*. One-sidedness is said to be bias in one place. Correctness is in moving about anywhere. The Correct Mind shows itself by extending the mind throughout the body. It is not biased in any one place.

When the mind is biased in one place and lacking in another, it is called a *one-sided mind*. One-sidedness is despicable. To be arrested by anything, no matter what, is falling into one-sidedness and is despised by those travelling the Way.

When a person does not think, "Where shall I put it?" the mind will extend throughout the entire body and move about to any place at all.

Not putting the mind anywhere, can't one use the mind, having it go from place to place, responding to the opponent's movements?

If the mind moves about the entire body, when the hand is called into action, one should use the mind that is in the hand. When the foot is called for, one should use the mind that is in the foot. But if you determine one place in which

31

to put it, when you try to draw it out of that place, there it will stay. It will be without function.

Keeping the mind like a tied-up cat and not allowing it to wander, when you keep it in check within yourself, within yourself will it be detained. Forsaking it within your body, it will go nowhere.

The effort not to stop the mind in just one place—this is discipline. Not stopping the mind is object and essence. Put nowhere, it will be everywhere. Even in moving the mind outside the body, if it is sent in one direction, it will be lacking in nine others. If the mind is not restricted to just one direction, it will be in all ten.

THE RIGHT MIND AND THE CONFUSED MIND

The Right Mind is the mind that does not remain in one place. It is the mind that stretches throughout the entire body and self.

The Confused Mind is the mind that, thinking something over, congeals in one place.

When the Right Mind congeals and settles in one place, it becomes what is called the Confused Mind. When the Right Mind is lost, it is lacking in function here and there. For this reason, it is important not to lose it.

In not remaining in one place, the Right Mind is like water. The Confused Mind is like ice, and ice is unable to wash hands or head. When ice is melted, it becomes water and flows everywhere, and it can wash the hands, the feet or anything else.

If the mind congeals in one place and remains with one thing, it is like frozen water and is unable to be used freely:

ice that can wash neither hands nor feet. When the mind is melted and is used like water, extending throughout the body, it can be sent wherever one wants to send it.

This is the Right Mind.

THE MIND OF THE EXISTENT MIND AND THE MIND OF NO-MIND

The Existent Mind is the same as the Confused Mind and is literally read as the "mind that exists." It is the mind that thinks in one direction, regardless of subject. When there is an object of thought in the mind, discrimination and thoughts will arise. Thus it is known as the Existent Mind.

The No-Mind is the same as the Right Mind. It neither congeals nor fixes itself in one place. It is called No-Mind when the mind has neither discrimination nor thought but wanders about the entire body and extends throughout the entire self.

The No-Mind is placed nowhere. Yet it is not like wood or stone. Where there is no stopping place, it is called No-Mind. When it stops, there is something in the mind. When there is nothing in the mind, it is called the mind of No-Mind. It is also called No-Mind-No-Thought.

When this No-Mind has been well developed, the mind does not stop with one thing nor does it lack any one thing. It is like water overflowing and exists within itself. It appears appropriately when facing a time of need.

The mind that becomes fixed and stops in one place does not function freely. Similarly, the wheels of a cart go around because they are not rigidly in place. If they were to stick tight, they would not go around. The mind is also something that does not function if it becomes attached to a single situation.

33

If there is some thought within the mind, though you listen to the words spoken by another, you will not really be able to hear him. This is because your mind has stopped with your own thoughts.

If your mind leans in the directions of these thoughts, though you listen, you will not hear; and though you look, you will not see. This is because there is something in your mind. What is there is thought. If you are able to remove this thing that is there, your mind will become No-Mind, it will function when needed, and it will be appropriate to its use.

The mind that thinks about removing what is within it will by the very act be occupied. If one will not think about it, the mind will remove these thoughts by itself and of itself become No-Mind.

If one always approaches his mind in this way, at a later date it will suddenly come to this condition by itself. If one tries to achieve this suddenly, it will never get there.

An old poem says:

> To think, "I will not think"—
> This, too, is something in one's thoughts.
> Simply do not think
> About not thinking at all.

THROW THE GOURD INTO THE WATER, PUSH IT DOWN AND IT WILL SPIN

Pushing down a gourd means to do it with your hand. When a gourd is thrown into the water and pressed down, it will suddenly pop up to one side. No matter what, it is a thing that will not stop in one place.

The mind of the man who has arrived does not stop at one thing even for a bit. It is like pushing down the gourd in the water.

ENGENDER THE MIND WITH NO PLACE TO ABIDE

In our Sino-Japanese way of writing, this is pronounced *ōmushojū jijōgoshin*.

Regardless of what a person does, when he engenders the mind that thinks about doing something, the mind stops in that thing. Therefore, one should engender the mind without a place for it to stop.

If the mind is not engendered, the hand will not move forward. Those who when moving engender the mind that ordinarily stops in that movement, but do not stop at all in the course of the action—these are called the accomplished men of all Ways.

The mind of attachment arises from the stopping mind. So does the cycle of transmigration. This stopping becomes the bonds of life and death.

One looks at cherry blossoms or autumn leaves, and while engendering the mind that is looking at them, it is essential not to stop with them.

Jien's poem goes:[9]

> The flower that would surrender its fragrance
> before my brushwood door
> Does so regardless.
> I, however, sit and stare—
> How rueful, this world.

This means that the flower gives off its fragrance with No-

Mind, while I stare at it, my mind going no further. How regrettable, that the mind has so impaled me.

Make it a secret principle in either seeing or hearing not to detain the mind in one place.

The word *seriousness* is elaborated on by the saying, "One aim with no distractions."[10] The mind is settled in one place and is not allowed elsewhere. Later, even if you unsheathe your sword to strike, it is considered essential not to allow the mind movement in the direction of the strike. Especially in such matters as receiving commands from your lord, one should keep the word *seriousness* in the mind's eye.

In Buddhism, we also have the mentality of seriousness. When a bell called the Bell of Reverence is rung three times, we place our hands together and do obeisance. This attitude of reverence, in which one first intones the name of the Buddha, is synonymous with having "one aim with no distractions" or "one mind without confusion."

In Buddhism the mentality of seriousness is not the deepest level. Grasping one's mind and not letting it become confused is the discipline of the novice just beginning to learn.

This practice, when applied for a long period of time, leads to advancement to the level of freedom in which one can let the mind go in any direction. The level mentioned above of "engendering the mind with no place to abide" is the highest level of all.

The meaning of the word *seriousness* is in holding the mind in check and not sending it off somewhere, thinking that if one did let it go, it would become confused. At this level there is a tightening up of the mind and not an iota of negligence is allowed.

This is like a baby sparrow being caught by a cat. To prevent a recurrence, a string is then always tightened around the cat, and it is never let go.

If my mind is treated like a tied-up cat, it will not be free and will likely not be able to function as it should. If the cat is well trained, the string is untied, and it is allowed to go wherever it pleases. Then, even if the two are together, the cat will not seize the sparrow. Acting along these lines is the meaning of the phrase "engendering the mind with no place for it to abide."

Letting go of my mind and ignoring it like the cat, though it may go where it pleases, this will be using the mind in the way of not having it stop.

If we put this in terms of your own martial art, the mind is not detained by the hand that brandishes the sword. Completely oblivious to the hand that wields the sword, one strikes and cuts his opponent down. He does not put his mind in his adversary. The opponent is Emptiness. I am Emptiness. The hand that holds the sword, the sword itself, is Emptiness. Understand this, but do not let your mind be taken by Emptiness.

When the Zen priest at Kamakura, Mugaku, was captured during the disturbances in China and was at the point of being cut down, he quoted the *gatha*, "With the speed of a flash of lightning, / Cut through the spring breeze," and the soldier threw down his sword and fled.[11]

Mugaku meant that in wielding the sword, in the infinitesimal time it takes lightning to strike, there is neither mind nor thought. For the striking sword, there is no mind. For myself, who is about to be struck, there is no mind. The attacker is Emptiness. His sword is Emptiness. I, who am about to be struck, am Emptiness.

37

If this is so, the man who strikes is not a man at all. The striking sword is not a sword. And for myself, the person who is about to be cut, in a flash of lightning, it will be like cutting through the breeze that blows across the spring sky. It is the mind that absolutely does not stop. And it is not likely that the sword will react to cutting through the wind.

Completely forget about the mind and you will do all things well.

When you dance, the hand holds the fan and the foot takes a step. When you do not forget everything, when you go on thinking about performing with the hands and the feet well and dancing accurately, you cannot be said to be skillful. When the mind stops in the hands and the feet, none of your acts will be singular. If you do not completely discard the mind, everything you do will be done poorly.

SEEK THE LOST MIND

This is a saying of Mencius. It means that one should seek out the lost mind and return it to himself.

If a dog, cat or cock has escaped and run off to some other place, one will look for it and return it to his house. Likewise, when the mind, the master of the body, has gone off on a wicked path, why do we not seek after it and restore it to ourselves? This is certainly most reasonable.

But there is also a saying of Shao K'ang-chieh's that goes, "It is essential to lose the mind."[12] This is quite different. The general drift is that when the mind is tied down, it tires, and like the cat, is unable to function as it should. If the mind does not stop with things, it will not be stained by them and will be used well. Let it alone to run off wherever it will.

Because the mind is stained and stopped by things, we are warned against letting this happen, and are urged to seek after it and to return it to ourselves. This is the very first stage of training. We should be like the lotus which is unstained by the mud from which it rises. Even though the mud exists, we are not to be distressed by this. One makes his mind like the well-polished crystal which remains unstained even if put in the mud. He lets it go where it wishes.

The effect of tightening up on the mind is to make it unfree. Bringing the mind under control is a thing done only in the beginning. If one remains this way all through life, in the end he will never reach the highest level. In fact, he will not rise above the lowest.

When one is in training, it is good to keep Mencius' saying, "Seek the lost mind," in mind. The ultimate, however, is within Shao K'ang-chieh's, "It is essential to lose the mind."

Among the sayings of the priest Chung-fêng was, "Be in possession of a mind that has been let go of."[13] The meaning of this is exactly the same as Shao K'ang-chieh's dictum saying we should let go of the mind. Its significance is in warning us not to search for the lost mind or to tie it down in one place.

Chung-fêng also said, "Make no provision for retreat." This means to have a mind that will not be altered. It means that a man should be mindful that, although he advance well once or twice, he should not retreat when tired or in unusual circumstances.

Throw a Ball into a Swift Current and It Will Never Stop

There is a saying, "Throw a ball into a swift current and it will never stop."[14]

This means that if you throw a ball into rapidly flowing water, it will ride the waves and never stop dead.

Sever the Edge Between Before and After

There is a saying, "Sever the edge between before and after." Not ridding the mind of previous moments, allowing traces of the present mind to remain—both are bad. This means one should cut right through the interval between previous and present. Its significance is in cutting off the edge between before and after, between now and then. It means not detaining the mind.

Water Scorches Heaven, Fire Cleanses Clouds

> Today, burn not the fields of Musashino.
> Both spouse and I lie hidden
>   in the grasses of spring.[15]

Someone has expressed the meaning of this poem in this way:

> As the white clouds come together,
> The morning glories already fade.

There is something I have thought about only to myself of which I should advise you. And, while I know that it is only my own questionable and humble opinion, I feel that this is the right moment, and so will write down that which I perceive.

Since you are a master in the martial arts without equal in past or present, you are most resplendent in rank, stipend and reputation. Waking or sleeping, you should not forget this great boon and in order to return this favor by day and by night, you should think only of fulfilling your loyalty.

Total loyalty is first in making your mind correct, disciplining your body, not splitting your thoughts concerning your lord by even a hairsbreadth, and in neither resenting or blaming others. Do not be neglectful of your daily work. At home, be filial, let nothing indecent occur between husband and wife, be correct in formality, do not love mistresses, sever yourself from the path of sensuality, be austere as a parent, and act according to the Way. In employing underlings, do not make distinctions on the basis of personal feelings. Employ men who are good and bind them to you, reflect on your own deficiencies, conduct the government of your province correctly, and put men who are not good at a distance.

In this way, good men will advance daily, and those who are not will naturally be influenced when they see their lord loving the good. Thus they will leave off evil and turn toward the good themselves.

In this way, both lord and retainer, upper and lower, will be good men, and when personal desire becomes thin and pride is abandoned, the province's wealth will be plenty, the people will be well ruled, children will commune with their parents, and superior and menial will work together as hands and feet. The province should then become peaceful on its own. This is the beginning of loyalty.

Such an absolutely single-minded soldier would probably be your predilection in whatever situation should arise, even if you had the command of hundreds of thousands of men. When the whole mind of the Thousand-Armed Kannon is correct, each of the thousand arms will be of use; in the same way, if the mind of your martial art is correct, the function of your whole mind will be free, and even a thousand foes would be at the mercy of your single sword. Is this not great loyalty?

Whether the mind is correct or not is indiscernible by other people. When any single thought arises, both good and evil are there. If one will think about the foundation of good and evil, and do good and refrain from evil, his mind will become correct of itself.

Knowing what is evil but not refraining from it is a sickness of one's own desires. Whether it be from a love of sensuality or self-indulgence, it is a matter of the mind desiring something. Then, even if a good man were present, his good would not be put to use if it didn't strike one's fancy. To be pleased once with an ignorant man, to take a liking to him, and to give him an appointment while not using the good man that is there, is the same as having no good men at all.

Even if one employed several thousand men, there is unlikely to be one who would stand in good stead to his lord in a time of emergency. As for the ignorant young evil men who were once so attractive, their hearts not being correct from the beginning, they would on no account be able to think of sacrificing their own lives when facing a real situation. I have never once heard, even in times past, of men whose minds were not correct standing in good stead to their lords.

The appearance that such a thing may happen when your

lordship chooses apprentices is a bitter shame indeed.

This is something that nobody knows: from some offbeat inclination, one may be pulled along into bad habits and fall into evil. While you may think that no one knows about these faults, as "there is nothing as clear as that which is dimly seen," if they are known in your own mind, they will also be known by heaven, earth, the gods and the people.[16] If such is the case, is the protection of the province not truly in danger? You should recognize this as great disloyalty.

For example, no matter how ardently you yourself proffer loyalty to your lord, if the people in your clan are not in harmony and the population of Yagyū Valley turn their backs on you, everything you do will come to naught.

It is said that, in all things, if you would know a man's good and evil points, you should know the retainers and underlings he loves and employs, and the friends with whom he mixes intimately. If the lord is not correct, none of his retainers and friends will be correct. If this is the case, he will be despised by all and the neighboring provinces will hold him in contempt. But if the lord and his retainers are good, they will be regarded fondly by all.

It is said that a good man is regarded as a jewel by the province. You should make this your own personal experience.

When in a place where people recognize you, if you will quickly avoid unrighteousness, put characterless people at a distance, and love the wise, the provincial government will become all the more correct and you will be the best of all loyal retainers.

Above all, concerning your honored son's behavior, it is going at things backwards to attack a child's wrongdoings if the parent himself is incorrect. If you will first make your own conduct correct and then voice your opinions, not only will he naturally correct himself, but his younger brother, Master Naizen, will learn from his conduct and become correct as well. Thus will father and sons become good men. This would be a happy outcome.

It is said that one takes men on or casts them off according to right-mindedness. At this time, as you are a favored retainer, it is absolutely unthinkable that bribes may be handsomely received from all the provincial lords, or that right-mindedness may be forgotten because of avarice.

That you enjoy *ranbu*, that you are prideful of your own ability in Nō, and that you push yourself in among the provincial lords showing off this ability, I earnestly believe to be a sickness.[17]

Shouldn't you reflect over and over again on the facts that the emperor's recitation is given like *Sarugaku*, and that the provincial daimyo first in courtesy are the ones most often brought before the shogun?[18]

In the song it says:

> It is the very mind itself
> That leads the mind astray;
> Of the mind,
> Do not be mindless.

The Clear Sound of Jewels

There is nothing dearer to us than life. Whether a man be rich or poor, if he does not live out a long life, he will not accomplish his true purpose. Even if one had to throw away thousands in wealth and valuables to do so, life is something he should buy.

It is said that life is of small account compared with right-mindedness.[1] In truth, it is right-mindedness that is most esteemed.

Nothing is more precious than life. Yet, at the moment when we must throw away this valued life and stand on right-mindedness, there is nothing more highly esteemed than right-mindedness.

Looking carefully at the world, we can see that there are many people who throw away their lives lightly. But do you suppose one person in a thousand would die for right-mindedness? It would seem that among the humble servant class, contrary to what you might expect, there are many who would. Yet it would be difficult for people who think themselves wise to do the same.

As I was saying such things half to myself while passing a long spring day, a certain man came up and said something like this:

"While wealth truly pleases our hearts, having life is the greatest wealth of all. So when it comes to the moment of reckoning, a man will throw away his wealth to keep his life intact. But when you think that a man will not hesitate to throw away the life he so values for the sake of right-mindedness, the value of right-mindedness is greater than life itself. Desire, life and right-mindedness—among these three, isn't the latter what man values most?"

At that time, I replied something along these lines.

"Desire, life and right-mindedness—to say that right-mindedness is the most valued among these three is only natural. But to say that all men without exception value right-mindedness the most among these three misses the mark. There is no man who simply values desire and life but keeps right-mindedness in his thoughts."

Then another man said, "Wealth is a jewel of life. Without life, wealth is useless, so life alone is valuable. However, it is said that there are many who lightly throw away their lives for right-mindedness."

I asked, "Is any man able to take his life lightly for the sake of right-mindedness?"

He responded, "There are many people in this world who cannot abide being insulted and who will quickly, along with their foes of the moment, throw away their lives in a fight. This is having right-mindedness foremost in mind and taking one's life lightly. It is dying for right-mindedness rather than for wealth or life.

"Those who were cut down in the face of battle—their number can hardly be known. All were men who died for right-mindedness. With this in mind, it can be said that all men value right-mindedness over desire and life."

I said, "Dying because someone is vexed at being insulted resembles right-mindedness, but it is not that at all. This is forgetting oneself in the anger of the moment. It is not right-mindedness in the least. Its proper name is anger and nothing else. Before a person has even been insulted, he has already departed from right-mindedness. And for this reason, he suffers insult. If one's right-mindedness is correct when he is associating with others, he will not be insulted by them. Being insulted by others, one should realize that he had lost his

48

own right-mindedness prior to the offense."

Right-mindedness is a matter of extreme importance. Its substance is none other than the Principle of Heaven, which gives life to all things. When this is acquired by the human body, it is called one's nature. Its other names are virtue, the Way, human-heartedness, probity and propriety. While the name changes according to the situation, and though its function is different, in substance it is only one thing.

When this is written as *human-heartedness* and the situation involves human intercourse, its function is benevolence.

When it is written as *right-mindedness* and the situation involves social station and integrity, its function is in making no mistakes in clarity of judgment.

Even in dying, if one has not hit upon the principle therein, he has no right-mindedness, albeit some think that if a person just dies, he had this quality.[2]

Right-mindedness is considered to be the substance devoid of perversity that is the core of the human mind; and in using the straightness in that core of the mind as a plumbline, everything produced will exhibit right-mindedness.

Disregarding this core and dying because of desire is not a right-minded death. As for those people we mentioned who die for right-mindedness, can there even be one in a thousand who would truly do so?

In regard to this, from the time one has been taken into a daimyo's service, of the clothes on his back, the sword he wears at his side, his footgear, his palanquin, his horse and all of his materiel, there is no single item that is not due to the favor of his lord. Family, wife, child and his own retainers—all of them and their relations—not one can be said not to receive the lord's favor. Having these favors well impressed on his mind, a man will face his lord's opponents on the battlefield and cast away his one life. This is dying for right-mindedness.

This is not for the sake of one's name. Nor for gaining fame, a stipend and a fief. Receiving a favor and returning a favor—the sincerity of the core of the mind consists solely of this.

Is there one person in a thousand who would die like this? If there were one person in a thousand, then there would be a hundred in a hundred thousand, and for any eventuality there would be a hundred thousand men available.

In truth, one hundred right-minded men would be hard to find.

Regardless of the epoch, whenever the country was in disorder, there might be five to seven thousand corpses after a battle. Among them were men who met the enemy and made names for themselves. Others were struck down by the enemy without anyone's noticing. All of these men would seem to have died for right-mindedness, but many of them did not. Many died for name and for profit.

The first thought is of doing something for fame; the second is to think of establishing a name, and later of receiving land and coming up in the world.

There are people who accomplish notable feats, attract fame and come up in the world. There are those who die in battle. There are among the older samurai those who would make a name for themselves in the next battle so as to leave it to their descendants in their old age; or if they did not die in battle, they would try to leave both name and estate. All these take their lives lightly, but all are concerned with name and profit. Theirs is a hot-blooded death born of desire. It is not right-mindedness.

Those who receive a kind word from their lord and devote their lives to him also die a death of right-mindedness. But there are none who value right-mindedness even though it is what should be valued most. So those who throw away their lives for desire, and those who hold their lives dear and expose themselves to shame belong with those who take right-mindedness lightly, whether they live or die.

Ch'eng Ying and Ch'u Chiu died together for the sake of right-mindedness.[3] Po I and Shu Ch'i were men who thought deeply about right-mindedness, and lamented the fact that a vassal would kill his own king.[4] In the end, they died of starvation at the foot of Mount Shouyang.

In seeking out men like these, we find there weren't many, even in antiquity. Even more so, in today's Wayless world, there are likely none who, valuing right-mindedness, would lightly toss aside both desire and life. Usually people throw away their lives for the sake of desire, or they hold their lives dear and cover themselves with shame. None know a hair's tip about right-mindedness.

All men put on the face of right-mindedness, but they do not truly think about it. Because of this folly, when some unpleasantness is visited upon a man, he is unable to bear it and spits out words of abuse. The object of these words is then mortified and proceeds to throw away his life in retaliation. This man is not only lacking in right-mindedness, he reeks of desire.

To think that I can perpetrate some unpleasantness on a man and avoid his verbal abuse—this is nothing but a manifestation of desire. It is the kind of passion involved when a man gives someone a rock and, if the person gives him gold in return, becomes his friend; but if the other gives him a rock in return, cuts off his head. When a man praises another in glowing terms, such words are likely to be returned to him as well. But when he slanders another and, the slander being given back in kind, cuts off the man's head and dies himself, this is desire. It is the opposite of right-mindedness and the height of stupidity.

Moreover, those who are samurai all have masters, and to throw away the life that should be given up for one's lord, dying for the sake of an argument, is not to know the difference between right and wrong. It is, above all, not to know the meaning of right-mindedness.

What is called desire is not simply attaching oneself to wealth, or thinking only about one's fancies for silver and gold.

When the eye sees colors, this is desire.

When the ear hears sounds, this is desire.

When the nose smells fragrances, this is desire.

When a single thought simply germinates, this is called desire.

This body has been solidified and produced by desire, and it is in the nature of things that all men have a strong sense of it. Although there is a desireless nature confined within this desire-firmed and produced body, it is always hidden by hot-bloodedness, and its virtue is difficult to sow. This nature is not protected easily. Because it reacts to the Ten Thousand Things in the external world, it is drawn back by the Six Desires, and submerges beneath them.[5]

This body is composed of the Five Skandhas: form, feeling, conception, volition and consciousness.

Form is the carnal body.

Feeling is the carnal body's sensing of good and evil, right and wrong, sorrow and joy, and pain and pleasure.

Conception means predilections. It is hating evil, desiring good, fleeing from sorrow, hoping for joy, avoiding pain and desiring pleasure.

Volition means operating the body on the basis of feeling and perception. This means hating pain and so obtaining pleasure, or hating evil and so doing things that are good for oneself.

Consciousness is discriminating the good and evil, right and wrong, pain and pleasure, and joy and sorrow of the above feeling, conception and volition. Through consciousness, evil is known to be evil, good to be good, pain to be pain, and pleasure to be pleasure.

Because consciousness discriminates and forms prejudices, it abhors the ugly and adheres to the beautiful, and according to its attachments, the carnal body moves.

Because the carnal body exists, there is the skandha of feeling.

Because the skandha of feelings exists, there is the skandha of conception.

Because the skandha of conception exists, it brings the skandha of volition into action.

Because the skandha of volition is brought into action, the skandha of consciousness exists.

Because of the skandha of consciousness, we discriminate between good and evil, right and wrong, and ugly and beautiful, thoughts arise concerning acceptance and rejection, and, just as these thoughts arise, the carnal body is born. This is like the sun or moon being reflected in puddles of water. The Buddha explained that "the manifestation of form in response to the material world is like the moon in the midst of the water."[6]

Form, feeling, conception, volition, consciousness—then from consciousness back to form—if these are condensed over and over again, the linkage of the Five Skandhas according to the flow of the Twelve Links in the Chain of Existence, having received this body, begins with a single thought of our consciousness.[7]

Consciousness is, therefore, desire. This desire, this consciousness, gives rise to this body of the Five Skandhas. As the entire body is something hardened by desire, when a single hair is pulled from the head, thoughts of desire will arise. When you are touched by the tip of a finger, thoughts of desire arise. Even when you are touched by the tip of a toenail, thoughts of desire arise. The entire body is solidified by desire.

Within this body solidified by desire is concealed the absolutely desireless and upright core of the mind. This mind is not in the body of the Five Skandhas, has no color or form, and is not desire. It is unwaveringly correct, it is absolutely straight. When this mind is used as a plumbline, anything done at all will be right-mindedness. This absolutely straight thing is the substance of right-mindedness.

Right-mindedness is a name added temporarily when it manifests itself in external affairs. It is also called *human-heartedness*. Benevolence is its function. When we indicate its substance, we say "human-heartedness"; benevolence is a designation we give it temporarily. Human-heartedness, right-mindedness, propriety, wisdom—the substance is the same, but the names are different.

These things should be understood as the core of the mind.

It is for this reason that the Way of Confucius is said to be that of sincerity and sympathy. *Sincerity* is the same as "the core of the mind." *Sympathy* is the same as "like mind" or "oneness." If the core of the mind and like-mindedness are achieved, not one in ten thousand affairs will ever turn out poorly.

Even though one may say such things, if a man has not been enlightened, you may explain for a hundred days and he may listen for a hundred days, but he is little likely to gain the Way.

If we speak thusly and there be those who deny what we say, it would be best to look at the innermost thoughts and actions of the people who lecture and listen to the Confucian Classics. It is no different with those who lecture and those who listen to the Buddhist scriptures. This is not just a criticism of Confucianism. A person may be as eloquent as a rushing stream, but if his mind has not been enlightened and if he has not seen into his own true nature, he will not be someone to be relied upon. We should be able to discern this quickly from a person's behavior.

A certain person expressed his doubts, saying, "If even the acts of seeing and hearing are desire, if even the raising of a single thought is desire, how will we be able to attain right-mindedness? The concentration of a single thought is like a rock or tree. Being like a rock or tree, one is not likely to act with right-mindedness for his master's sake. If one does not actuate a strong sense of willpower, it will be difficult to accomplish."

I said, "This is a justifiable doubt. With no thoughts in the mind, one will run neither to the right nor to the left, will climb neither up nor down, but will go only straight ahead.

55

When a single thought just barely arises, one will run to the right or left, climb up or down, and finally arrive at the place of his desire. This is why it is called desire.

"The virtue of the unwaveringly correct is hidden. If this desire is not put into action, one is not likely to achieve either good or evil. Even if you have a mind to rescue a man who has fallen into an abyss, if you have no hands, you will not be able to do so. Again, if a man has a mind to push someone into an abyss, if he has no hands, he will not be able to do so. In this way, whether it be success or failure, as soon as there are hands that bring about success or failure, the nature of things is departed from.

"One borrows the strength of desire while either succeeding or failing, and when he considers the unwaveringly correct and straight mind to be his plumbline and acts according to it, success and failure are still matters of that strength.

"But if one does not stray from this plumbline, it is not called desire. It is called right-mindedness. Right-mindedness is none other than virtue.

"Consider the core of the mind to be a wagon, with will-power to be carried about in it. Push it to a place where there can be failure, and there will be failure. Push it to a place where there can be success, and there will be success. But whether there is success or failure, if one entrusts himself to the straightness of this wagon of the core of the mind, he will attain right-mindedness in either case. Severing oneself from desire and being like a rock or tree, nothing will ever be achieved. Not departing from desire, but realizing a desireless right-mindedness—this is the Way."

Among the gods, there are those who are famous and those who are unknown. Sumiyoshi, Tamatsushima, Kitano and

Hirano are all famous gods. When we simply speak of the gods, we mean the ones whose names we do not know. When we speak of worshipping and revering the gods, we do not make distinctions among the names of Sumiyoshi, Tamatsushima, Hirano and Kitano. We worship and revere the gods regardless of who they are.

When the god of Kitano is worshipped, the god of Hirano is left aside. If the god of Hirano is being revered, Kitano is put aside.

Limiting one god to one location, the other gods are not considered to be of value. This particular god is revered exclusively, or this one is worshipped and the other discarded.

When we speak of the gods, we do not limit them, one god to one place. This would not be establishing the Way of the Gods. The Way of the Gods is established when we worship the gods, no matter where we are or what god we may be facing. We should speak of this in connection with the Way of Lord and Retainer.

Lord means the emperor and *retainer* means the retainers of the emperor. *Lord* and *retainer* are not words used for people below these in rank, but for the present we will use them in that way.

Among the lords, there are those who are famous and those whose names are unknown. Among retainers as well, there are likely those who are famous and those who are not. In speaking of a famous lord, a man will say something like, "Our lord is Matsui Dewa," or "My lord is Yamamoto Tajima." In speaking of unknown lords, one simply says, "the lord," without mentioning his name.

For a man who is a retainer, the Way of the Lord should be established if he will simply think, "the lord." And for the lord, if he will simply think "the retainer," the Way of the Retainer should be established.

Long ago it was said that "a wise retainer does not serve two lords." This meant that it was thought that a retainer would never have two masters. The world being in decline, retainers now employ themselves under this lord and that, in the end fitting the image of vagabond attendants while proclaiming their own merits. Such are the times in which we live.

A lord, saying that he is not pleased with one man or another, will drive the man from the household and heap shame upon him. This also puts the Way of Lord and Retainer, Master and Servant, in disorder.

Even if a retainer does serve in a number of clans, he should think of his master as being the one and only. This means that the lord will be an unknown lord, for, if he is unknown, the Way of the Lord will be established. Even if he serves in clan after clan, he should think of that lord as "the lord," and this lord as "the lord." In this way he will think of the lord with great devotion and, even though the clan may change, his mind will not. Thus, the lord will be the one and only from beginning to end.

If a man thinks, "My lord is Matsui Dewa, but he is really a lout. . . ." while he is receiving a stipend or fief and coming up in the world, his mind will not be thinking "the lord" at all. When he next employs himself under Lord Yamamoto Tajima, the same mind will follow along with him. Thus, no matter where he goes, he will never understand the meaning of the word *lord* and is not likely to prosper.

Therefore it is better not to inquire who this lord or that might be, but to simply think "the lord," and to consider right-mindedness towards him without mentioning his name. If this is done, and if one serves this lord with thoughts of never stepping in front of the man or even treading on his shadow the entire time he is receiving his support, whether it be one month, one year or even ten years, though he serve in many clans, the lord will be only one.

The lord, though there be a turnover of retainers, should not meddle with the Way of the Retainer. He should have love and sympathy deep in his heart, should not make distinctions between newcomers and old-timers, and should act with great charity towards all. In this way, the retainers will all be without names, the lord will be without name, and the Way of Lord and Retainer, Master and Servant, will be established. There should be no distinctions made between the new retainer who just began serving today and the old-timers who have been employed for ten to twenty years. All men should be treated with love and sympathy, and each man should be thought of as "My retainer."

It is likely that stipend and fief will differ considerably, but there should be no distinctions within the mind of human-heartedness and love. Even if a retainer has just begun his employment today, the meaning of thinking "the lord" will not be found in thinking "today's lord."

Is not this the Way of Lord and Retainer?

Li Po said:

Heaven and earth are the wayfarer's inn of the Ten Thousand Things. Fleeting time is the traveler of a hundred generations. This floating life is like a dream.[8] How long will our happiness last? The ancients lit lamps and amused themselves at night. Truly there was a reason for this.

Things does not mean only those things without sentience; it is said that man is a thing.[9] The space between heaven and earth is the inn for the travelling back and forth of both men and things. In the end, there is no standing still for either men or things. The passing of time is like the unending passing of the traveller, and the gradual passing of spring, summer, fall and winter has not changed for a hundred generations.

The body is like a dream. When we see this and awake, not a trace remains. How much time is left for the looking?

It was not without reason that the ancients went from night to day, lighting the lamps and amusing themselves throughout the hours of darkness.

At this point, one could fall into error. There should be standards for amusement, and if there are, amusement will bear no evil. The person who has no standards will become insane. If the one amusing himself does not fall into error, he will not go beyond these standards. What we mean by standards are generally fixed limits in regards to all things. Like the joints in bamboo, amusement, for the most part, should have limits. It is not good to go beyond them.

The court nobility has the amusements of the court, the samurai class has the amusements of the samurai, and the priests have the amusements of the priests. Each should have their amusements accordingly.

It could be said that involvement in amusements unbecoming to one's station is erring in one's standards. For the court nobility, there is Chinese and Japanese poetry and the wind and stringed instruments. With these, they will pass from night to day and there should be nothing wrong. It is reasonable that the samurai class and the priests, too, should each have their own appropriate amusements.

Strictly speaking, for priests there shouldn't be such things as amusements. It is said, however, that "In public, not even a needle can enter, but in private, both horse and cart pass right through."[10] This means that, sympathizing with the mind of man and recognizing that the world has degenerated, we should probably allow them to have their own amusements as well. While meeting in the seclusion of night, they should be allowed to compose Chinese and Japanese poetry. Even linked verse should be appropriate. On another level, it is not unfitting for them to lean their hearts towards the moon and cherry blossoms and, accompanied by fourteen- or fifteen-year-old youths, to go to a place where the moon can be viewed from beneath the blossoms, a tasteful sake jar in hand, and share some cups with them. To have a small inkstone and writing paper would not be at all in bad taste.

But even these are not considered correct for a priest who would have a religious spirit. Much less, the other unrefined entertainments.

It would not be surprising if the nobility and the samurai alike, when they realized that this floating world is but a dream, lit the lamps and amused themselves throughout the night.

There are those who say, "Everything is like a dream! The only thing to do is play!" These people rattle their minds beyond limit, sink themselves in pleasure, and go to the extremes of luxury. Though they quote the words of the men of old, they are as far from the minds of the ancients as snow is from soot.

When Ippen Shōnin met Hottō Kokushi, the founder of the Kōkokuji in the village of Yura in Kii Province, he said, "I have composed a poem."[11]

Kokushi said, "Let's hear it."
Shōnin recited:

> When I chant,
> Both Buddha and self
> Cease to exist.
> There is only the voice that says,
> *Namu Amida Butsu.*[12]

Kokushi said, "Something's wrong with the last couple of lines, don't you think?"

Shōnin then confined himself in Kumano and meditated for twenty-one days. When he passed by Yura again, he said, "This is how I've written it":

> When I chant,
> Both Buddha and self
> Cease to exist.
> *Namu Amida Butsu,*
> *Namu Amida Butsu.*

Kokushi nodded his enthusiastic approval and said, "There! You got it!"

This was written down in Kogaku Oshō's notes.[13] We should look at this again and again.

I will speak about the Ten Essential Qualities.[14] They are Form, Nature, Embodiment, Power, Function, Latent Cause, External Cause, Latent Effect, Manifest Effect and Total Inseparability of one from the others. The Ten Worlds are those of Hell, Hunger, Animality, Anger, Humankind, Heaven, Learning, Realization, Bodhisattvahood and Buddhahood.[15] The Ten Essential Qualities are like these. Generally, from the Worlds of Hell, Hunger, Animality, Anger, Humankind and Heaven to the Worlds of Learning, Realization, Bodhisattvahood and Buddhahood, all are possessed of the Ten Essential Qualities.[16]

As a rule, a thing born cannot be without Form, so we speak of the Essential Quality of Form. Although Form may change in multitudinous ways, as Form it is the same. When the Form changes, even the sound of its song will change: the cuckoo sings the song of the cuckoo, the nightingale sings the song of the nightingale.

Does each of these, to express its own form, change its shape even to the extent of the song it sings? Certainly the cuckoos in the mountains and the nightingales of the valley recite their own songs. But we should not take this to mean that even the sound changes if the form changes. Song is something that makes its context more refined, and the context of words is something we combine with right-mindedness and come to know it thereby.

If something has Form, it will also have a Nature. Although the Buddha-nature is always the same, Form follows whatever receives it, and thus changes.

All sentient beings have the Buddha-nature, and so even those in Hell, and in the Worlds of Hunger and Animality are unchanging in this. It is explained in this way, even in the sutras.

If a number of mirrors are placed around a pedestal and a single lamp is placed in the center, the lamp will be seen in each of the mirrors. The lamp is only one, but is reflected in each of the mirrors. This exemplifies the Buddha-nature being only one, yet being received by all sentient beings of the Ten Worlds, even by the hungry and by animals. This is the example of the mirror and the lamp in The Flower Garland Sutra.[17]

Embodiment means the Embodiment of the Law. In all the Ten Thousand Things there are both Embodiment and Function. Form is born of Embodiment; then, having gone its full round, it perishes. Embodiment itself is never exhausted.

Let us say that snow and ice are Function, and that water is Embodiment. When water solidifies, it becomes ice, but then melts again and becomes the original water. Consider water as Embodiment.

This is an example of the manifestation of Embodiment when the ten thousand Forms are born from the Embodiment of the Law and then perish.

The ordinary man is unable to see beyond Form. He is unable to see Embodiment. When something is produced, he says it has manifested itself. From the standpoint of enlightenment, we say it has manifested itself when it has returned to Embodiment and can no longer be seen.

> The snow at the peaks,
> The ice at the mountain depths
> Melt and raise
> The sound in the foothills:
> The water of spring.

This is written about Embodiment.

If a thing is possessed of Form, Nature and Embodiment, it must also have Power. Power is the strength to be able to function efficaciously; it is the strength behind the achievement of all phenomena. Concerning all things, what achieves effect is Power.

The constancy of the always green pine in the midst of luxuriantly green leaves on the summer mountain is especially well known in song. This is because it does not change its color in either frost or in late autumn showers. It remains constant even during the coldest part of the year and so is sung about and regarded as the Essential Quality of Power.

Because there is Power, Function accords performance to all things. If one goes on without slackening his efforts, learning one Chinese character today and another tomorrow, he should be able to achieve anything. The meaning of Function should be understood through the saying, "The journey of a thousand miles begins with a single step."

Given Form, Nature, Embodiment, Power and Function, no matter what is done, it can be done at will. This is Latent Cause. If something is not done, it is to one's own detriment, and there is nothing that cannot be done. Without both Latent Cause and External Cause, one will not likely get as far as the state of Buddhahood.[18]

The Chinese character for Latent Cause, for instance, is also read as "to depend on." This means that "depending on" one thing, various other things are obtained.

Planting the seed in the ground in spring is said to be the Latent Cause. And, though one has planted it firmly, if there is no help from the rain and dew, nothing will grow. The help of the rain and dew is said to be the External Cause. Depending on the help of the rain and dew, the plant will grow and there will be fruit in the fall. This is Latent Effect.

> When the heart is filled
> And will not be put at rest,
> My hopes will be
> After a thousand sheaths
> Of the honeysuckle vine.[19]

The meaning of this is that the setting up of the honeysuckle is the Latent Cause of getting married. Furthermore, the intermediation is said to be the External Cause, and, in the end, the couple becoming man and wife and prospering with children could be said to be an example of Latent Effect.

In the same way, if one would become a Buddha, if he does not first act in accordance with the Latent Cause, he will not reach the state of Buddhahood. Make discipline the Latent Cause, and later you will obtain the effect.

The word *effect* carries the meaning of "fruit." Depending on the planting of the Latent Cause in spring, one obtains the fruit in the fall. This is an example of the state of Buddhahood.

External Cause is seen in the above notes.

> The ship under sail
> Has surely passed
> The Cape of Wada,
> Driven as it is
> By the mountain winds of Muko.

The ship is the Latent Cause. The wind is the External Cause. Arriving at the other shore is the Latent Effect. Without the ship, one cannot reach the other shore. And, even though the ship exists, one cannot be without the External Cause of the wind. This is said to be the harmony of Latent Cause and External Cause. The mountain winds of Muko should be considered to be the External Cause. If one would become a Buddha, he cannot do without the discipline of the Latent Cause.

> Because I planted them,
> I can see their ripening

> At the ends of the branches,
> Branches grown thick
> With the pears at Iki Bay.

This is Latent Effect.

Obtaining the state of Buddhahood is like planting pear trees and then watching them grow.

> At the Bay of Iki
> On branches grown thick
> With pears that ripen,
>   with pears that do not;
> Are they not faithful
> Even in sleep?

This is the original poem. Iki Bay is in Ise.

Manifest Effect

> Wait and see!
> When you who treat others
> So cruelly try to love
> You will surely know
> (The way I feel.)

This love poem means, "Even though you treat me so cruelly, you are certainly not without love yourself. Perhaps you will come to know what love is. At that time you will get your reward."

If you do good in this life, you will be rewarded with good in the next. If you do evil, you will be rewarded with evil. This is Manifest Effect. If the Latent Cause is good, the Latent Effect will be good. If the Latent Cause is evil, the Latent Effect will be evil. It is like an echo responding to a voice, or a shadow accompanying a form.

That one disciplines himself with the Latent Cause in one life and obtains the reward in the next is natural. But there are also occasions of a present Latent Cause accompanied by a present Manifest Effect, a Latent Cause in the past followed by a present Manifest Effect, and a Latent Cause in the present followed by a Manifest Effect in the future. It goes from one world to the next, appearing sooner or later, and is something that cannot be avoided. There is also such a thing as simultaneous Latent Cause and Effect.

We can make an example with the flower as the Latent Cause and the fruit as the Manifest Effect. On a melon, the flower and fruit grow at the same time. With the rice plant, the fruit—or rather grain—grows, and the flower blossoms on its crown. Such things can be taken as examples.

Total Inseparability. From the Essential Quality of Form to the Essential Quality of Manifest Effect, there is no violation of Beginning to End. They go around and around from Root to Branch and are called the Ten Points. The Very Extremity means going to the very ultimate. This is, of course, the Ten Worlds. All living things—even the little worms— are possessed of these Ten Essential Qualities. Even the inanimate are not different from this.

Let's take examples from the fruits of the chestnut and the persimmon. To say that these have neither pain nor sorrow is to judge from the view of mankind. It can be seen that they are naturally outfitted with both pain and sadness.

The appearance of pain in grasses and trees is no different from the countenance of suffering among human beings. When they are watered and the like, they grow and appear happy. When they are cut and fall, the withering of their leaves is no different from the death of a human being.

Their pain and sadness are not known to human beings. And when grasses and trees look at the sadness of human beings, it is just like human beings looking at them, and they probably think we have no pain or sadness either. Simply, it seems that we do not know the affairs of grasses and trees, nor do they know ours. This is written in the books of the Confucianists.

When there are fences or roofed mud walls on the north side of growing plants, those plants will lean towards the south. Observing this, it is clear that plants know what is harmful to them, although they do not have eyes.

Sleeping at night and opening during the day, the lily is another example we could use. However, it is not the lily alone, but all grasses and trees that do not lack this nature.

It is because we do not pay attention that we pass along unknowing. Those who know completely about grasses and trees are sages. We do not understand these things because of our rough and conforming minds.

Whether something is sentient or insentient is calculated roughly. There is probably nothing in existence that is not sentient. Don't we say they are insentient because they lack the fashion of the things that are?

It is said that when a chicken is cold, it will fly up into the trees; when a duck is cold, it will swim in the water. Isn't this like thinking that, because a duck swims in the water when it is cold, it has no sense of cold, or because a chicken flies up into the trees when it is cold, it has no sense of cold, either?

Water is cold, and this is said to be its nature. Fire is hot, and this is considered to be its nature. From the standpoint of fire, water has no nature; from the standpoint of water, fire has no nature. Although it could be thought of in this way, in fact, they both have their own natures. We cannot say that anything is without its nature.

If we observe phenomena closely, it cannot be thought that anything between heaven and earth is really different. If we see differences, it is due to the narrowness of our vision.

This is like Mount Fuji's being concealed by a tree thick with branches and leaves, and my not being able to see it. But how can Mount Fuji be concealed by a single tree? It is simply because of the narrowness of my vision and because the tree stands in the way of my vision that Mount Fuji cannot be seen. We go on thinking that the tree is concealing Mount Fuji. Yet it is due to the narrowness of my vision.

Not understanding the principle of things, people often put on knowing faces and criticize those who do understand. And while they seem to be laughing at others, they are really laughing at themselves. At least those who truly understand must think so.

Look with real attention at the way the world is now. The earth is a mother and heaven a father. If we lodge the seed of the chestnut or the persimmon in the earth, the sprout appears and the fruit of the original chestnut or persimmon comes forth unchanged. In this way, it is brought up by a father and mother. Saying that it is lodged indicates that it is something brought in from another place.

For the human being, too, earth is mother and heaven is father, and the phenomenon that becomes the child is something brought in and lodged from another place.

What is called meta-existence is not the least bit different from thinking of things in this present existence. For this reason, this present existence is also called "an existence."

When this present existence comes to an end, there is what is called *meta-existence*. Then, meta-existence is altered and there is later-existence, or reincarnation. In any of these, there is absolutely no change in the mind that is in this present body.

Although there is a body even in meta-existence, it cannot be seen by human eyes because of its dimness. As for the meta-existence of those who were deeply attached to this world, there are cases of people having seen them. Since this is something that is out of the ordinary, people doubt these events and either blame them on the transformations of foxes and raccoon dogs, or explain them as illusory visions of the dead.

Both of the above situations are apt to occur as well. Admitting this, we should not dispose of each and every case as either one or the other. Real things also exist in this world. Such things are not just in the mouths of men. They have also been left by the pens of those who lived in the World of the Way and who were men of the Way themselves. When we do not measure up to the wisdom of the men who wrote these things, we should understand that we will have doubts.

When we see things in the middle of a dream, although we do not see and hear them with the eyes and ears given to us at birth, we distinctly meet people, say things, hear things, see colors, and even have sexual relations. We wrestle with the things that concern us daily, and, just as we think we are going to resolve our desires, wake up.

It is upon awakening that we realize it was a dream. In the dream itself we never think, "This is a dream" or "This is not real."

During a dream, this body is still alive and bound and cannot go to the places it would like. But with the strength of its own thoughts, it is able to see those places by drawing them to itself.

When one truly dies and leaves his own body, he goes where he wants to go like a cat released from a string. Although one's thoughts are the same as the thoughts in a dream, it is now as though he can go freely wherever he likes.

In the midst of profound darkness or when the doors and windows are shut, one enters a state of freedom. This is because he has no form.

In this case, although there is a form, there is no corporality, and it is like seeing the reflection of a lamp or the moon on the water. There are no hindrances.

This body acting as a barrier, one cannot enter the innermost shrine, but the mind can be conversant with that which is within, just as thoughts can pass through the Mountain of Silver or the Wall of Iron.[20] It is unlikely this mystery will be understood by the common run of men.

The Buddha and patriarchs understood this, but the common people do not know it at all. Not knowing it, they have doubts, and foolishness is added to foolishness.

There are any number of things I do not know and, not knowing them, I simply say they do not exist. Let's say I know six or seven things out of a hundred. When spoken to about those remaining, if I say they do not exist, then ninety things have ceased to be. But if I know fifteen or so, among those things that did not exist before, five or six more have come into existence. For those people who know twenty or thirty things, the number of non-existent things has decreased to only seventy. If one knows sixty or seventy out of a hundred, the remaining thirty or forty become just like those just mentioned. And when one knows all these things and thinks that there is nothing he does not know, it is because he is still unknowing.

If a man advances, making things clear one after another, he should be able to know all things. If there is something one knows, no one is likely to say that it does not exist, but if someone does it will be because he himself is ignorant of the matter.

A man who is extremely foolish should come to know something in the end because of his faith. On the other hand, isn't it said that "A half-baked martial art is the foundation of great injury"?

I understand that the Five Roots do not survive into meta-existence.[21] At that time the Five Roots of our present existence are transferred to the sixth sense of Consciousness. The Five Roots then have no form, but they continue to function.

As the sixth sense of Perception is consciousness, it has no form.[22] But because it has the faculties of seeing and hearing, in the middle of a dream while the physical eyes and ears do not help out, a different form is produced and seeing and hearing take place. It is called Consciousness because, although such and such a form does not exist, its function does.

If the form does not exist and it is something we cannot know, it is better just to say "seeing" or "hearing." Because seeing and hearing are transferred to Consciousness and have gone to a second level, the forms of the Five Roots are discarded and their functions are carried by Consciousness.

Although the Five Roots do not exist in meta-existence,

discernment of the five senses is no different from that in this present existence. One simply cannot see this from the outside. For the person involved, it is just like this present world. Moreover, even if the existence of the body were not denied, it is so vague that it is difficult to see.

When a bird flies through an empty sky, it becomes less clear as it gets farther away, and we come to think of it as having disappeared. Although we have lost sight of the form, it is not a matter of the bird's form vanishing and no longer existing. We do not see it because it has become too dim.

His form being weak and not clearly seen, we do not see a person in meta-existence. A person in this state can see us just as he did when living, but people do not know this.

When people who committed serious sins are in meta-existence, their forms are apparent. People see this naturally and call them ghosts and the like. Again, this is not something that does not exist. If people were deeply attached in this world, their forms are not weak at all.

It is like boiling up a broth from many things to make medicine. If the ingredients are weak, the broth will be weak. If the ingredients are thick, the broth will be thick. What is used for the broth will clearly be known. A very thin broth will be just like water. If it is just like water, people will not know it to be broth, but will view it simply as water.

In meta-existence, the form of a person who was deeply attached is apparent. But the person whose form is weak is the same as thin air, and we cannot see him. We cannot see him, but he can see us.

Because I have form, I can be seen. Because their forms are dim, I am unable to see them. In the *Ming-i Chi*, this is exemplified by the grain of barley.[23]

74

With a single grain of barley, the bud sprouts, and although it is endowed with the same functions as the original barley, if water and earth do not unify, it will not become barley at all.

Human consciousness and the objective world unite, sundry thoughts are born, and from these many others are born in turn. Pulled by these thoughts, this body of form is received and produced. It is not simply something strange that has rained down from heaven.

Beginning with the single thought that has no beginning, the multifarious things thus come to be. When you go and look carefully for its source, being a single thought with no beginning, you find that it has none at all. Having no origin at all, the birth of the infinite variety of things could be called a mystery.

Annals of
the Sword Taia

Presumably, as a martial artist, I do not fight for gain or loss, am not concerned with strength or weakness, and neither advance a step nor retreat a step. The enemy does not see me. I do not see the enemy. Penetrating to a place where heaven and earth have not yet divided, where Ying and Yang have not yet arrived, I quickly and necessarily gain effect.[1]

Presumably indicates something I do not know for sure. Originally, this character was read with the meaning "lid." For example, when a lid is put on a tier of boxes, although we do not know for sure what has been put inside, if we use our imaginations we will hit the mark six or seven times out of ten. Here also I do not know for sure, but figure tentatively that it must be so. Actually, this is a written form we use even about things we do know for sure. We do this to humble ourselves and so as not to seem to be speaking in a knowing manner.

Martial artist is as the characters indicate.

Not to fight for gain or loss, not to be concerned with strength or weakness means not vying for victory or worrying about defeat, and not being concerned with the functions of strength or weakness.

Neither advance a step nor retreat a step means taking neither one step forward nor one step to the rear. Victory is gained without stirring from where you are.

The *me* of "the enemy does not see me" refers to my True Self. It does not mean my perceived self.

People can easily see the perceived self; it is rare for them to discern the True Self. Thus I say, "The enemy does not see me."

I do not see the enemy. Because I do not take the personal view of the perceived self, I do not see the martial art of the enemy's perceived self.[2] Although I say, "I do not see the enemy," this does not mean I do not see the enemy right before my very eyes. To be able to see the one without seeing the other is a singular thing.

Well then, the True Self is the self that existed before the division of heaven and earth and before one's father and mother were born. This self is the self within me, the birds and the beasts, the grasses and the trees and all phenomena. It is exactly what is called the Buddha-nature.

This self has no shape or form, has no birth, and has no death. It is not a self that can be seen with the aid of your present physical eye. Only the man who has received enlightenment is able to see this. The man who does see this is said to have seen into his own nature and become a Buddha.

Long ago, the World Honored One went into the Snowy Mountains, and after passing six years in suffering, became enlightened.[3] This was the enlightenment of the True Self. The ordinary man has no strength of faith, and does not know the persistence of even three or five years. But those who study the Way are absolutely diligent for ten to twenty years, twenty-four hours a day. They muster up great strength of faith, speak with those who have wisdom, and disregard adversity and suffering. Like a parent who has lost a child, they do not retreat a scintilla from their established resolution. They think deeply, adding inquiry to inquiry. In the end, they arrive at the place where even Buddhist doctrine and the Buddhist Law melt away, and are naturally able to see "This."

Penetrating to a place where heaven and earth have not

yet divided, where Ying and Yang have not yet arrived, I quickly and necessarily gain effect means to set one's eye on the place that existed before heaven became heaven and earth became earth, before Ying and Yang came into being. It is to use neither thought nor reasoning and to look straight ahead. In this way, the time of gaining great effect will surely arrive.

> Well then, the accomplished man uses the sword but does not kill others. He uses the sword and gives others life. When it is necessary to kill, he kills. When it is necessary to give life, he gives life. When killing, he kills in complete concentration; when giving life, he gives life in complete concentration. Without looking at right and wrong, he is able to see right and wrong; without attempting to discriminate, he is able to discriminate well. Treading on water is just like treading on land, and treading on land is just like treading on water. If he is able to gain this freedom, he will not be perplexed by anyone on earth. In all things, he will be beyond companions.

The accomplished man means the man accomplished in the martial arts.

He uses the sword, but not to kill others means that even though he does not use the sword to cut others down, when others are confronted by this principle, they cower and become as dead men of their own accord. There is no need to kill them.

He uses the sword and gives others life means that while he deals with his opponent with a sword, he leaves everything to the movements of the other man, and is able to observe him just as he pleases.

When it is necessary to kill, he kills; when it is necessary to give life, he gives life. When killing, he kills with complete concentration; when giving life, he gives life with complete concentration means that in either giving life or taking life, he does so with freedom in a meditative state that is total absorption, and the meditator becomes one with the object of meditation.

Without looking at right and wrong, he is able to see right and wrong; without attempting to discriminate, he is able to discriminate well. This means that concerning his martial art, he does not look at it to say "correct" or "incorrect," but he is able to see which it is. He does not attempt to judge matters, but he is able to do so well.

If one sets up a mirror, the form of whatever happens to be in front of it will be reflected and will be seen. As the mirror does this mindlessly, the various forms are reflected clearly, without any intent to discriminate this from that. Setting up his whole mind like a mirror, the man who employs the martial arts will have no intention of discriminating right from wrong, but according to the brightness of the mirror of his mind, the judgment of right and wrong will be perceived without his giving it any thought.

Treading on water is just like treading on land, and treading on land is just like treading on water. The meaning of this will not be known by anyone unenlightened about the very source of mankind.

If the fool steps on land like he steps on water, when he walks on land, he is going to fall on his face. If he steps on water like he steps on land, when he does step onto water, he may think he can actually walk around. Concerning this matter, the man who forgets about both land and water should arrive at this principle for the first time.

If he is able to gain this freedom, he will not be perplexed by anyone on earth. According to this, the martial artist who is able to gain freedom will not be in a quandary about what to do, regardless of who on earth he comes up against.

In all things, he will be beyond companions means that as he will be without peer in all the world, he will be just like Shakyamuni, who said, "In Heaven above and Earth below, I alone am the Honored One."[4]

> Do you want to obtain this? Walking, stopping, sitting or lying down, in speaking and in remaining quiet, during tea and during rice, you must never neglect exertion, you must quickly set your eye on the goal, and investigate thoroughly, both coming and going. Thus should you look straight into things. As months pile up and years pass by, it should seem like a light appearing on its own in the dark. You will receive wisdom without a teacher and will generate mysterious ability without trying to do so. At just such a time, this does not depart from the ordinary, yet it transcends it. By name, I call it "Taia."

Do you want to obtain this? "This" points out what was written about above, so the question is whether you are considering obtaining the meaning of the foregoing.

Walking, stopping, sitting or lying down. The four of these—walking, stopping, sitting, lying down—are called the Four Dignities.[5] All people are involved in them.

In speaking and in remaining silent means while talking about things or without uttering a word.

During tea and during rice means while drinking tea and eating rice.

You must never neglect exertion, you must quickly set your eye on the goal, and investigate thoroughly, both coming and going. Thus should you look straight into things. This means that you should never be careless or negligent in your efforts, and you should constantly come back to yourself. You should quickly fix your eye on the goal and continually investigate these principles in depth. Always go straight ahead, considering what is right to be right, and what is wrong to be wrong, while observing this principle in all things.

As months pile up and years pass by, it should seem like a light appearing on its own in the dark means that, in just that way, you should carry on with your efforts tirelessly. As you advance with the accumulation of months and years, the acquiring you do on your own of this mysterious principle will be just like suddenly encountering the light from a lantern on a dark night.

You will receive wisdom without a teacher means that you will acquire this fundamental wisdom without its ever having been transmitted to you by a teacher.

You will generate mysterious ability without trying to do so. Because the works of the ordinary man all come from his consciousness, they are all actions of the world of created phenomena, and are involved with suffering. At the same time, because actions that are uncreated are generated from this fundamental wisdom, they alone are natural and peaceful.[6]

At just such a time means precisely at such a time. It indicates the time when one receives wisdom without a teacher and generates mysterious ability without trying to do so.

The meaning of *this does not depart from the ordinary, yet it transcends it* is that this uncreated mysterious ability is not generated from the unusual.

Since only actions that are unremarkably everyday in character become the uncreated, this principle never departs, nor does it separate itself, from the ordinary. Which is still to say that the ordinary actions in the world of created phenomena of the everyday ordinary man are entirely different. Thus it is said that "this does not depart from the ordinary, yet it transcends it."

By name, I call it "Taia." Taia is the name of an [ancient Chinese] sword that has no equal under heaven. This famous jewelled sword can freely cut anything, from rigid metal and tempered steel to dense and hardened gems and stones. Under heaven there is nothing that can parry this blade. The person who obtains this uncreated mysterious ability will not be swayed by the commander of huge armies or an enemy force of hundreds of thousands. This is the same as there being nothing that can impede the blade of this famous sword. Thus I call the strength of this mysterious ability the Sword Taia.

All men are equipped with this sharp Sword Taia, and in each one it is perfectly complete. Those for whom this is clear are feared even by the Maras, but those for whom this is obscure are deceived even by the heretics.[7] On the one hand, when two of equal skill meet at swords' point, there is no conclusion to the match; it is like Shakyamuni's holding the flower and Kashyapa's subtle smile.[8] On the other hand, raising the one and understanding the other three, or distinguishing subtle differences in weight with the unaided eye are examples of ordinary cleverness.[9] If anyone has mastered this, he will quickly cut you into three pieces even before the one has been raised and the three understood. How much more so when you meet him face to face?

All men are equipped with this sharp Sword Taia, and in each one it is perfectly complete. This means that the famous Sword Taia, which no blade under heaven can parry, is not imparted just to other men. Everyone, without exception, is equipped with it, it is inadequate for no one, and it is perfectly entire.

This is a matter of the mind. This mind was not born with your birth and will not die with your death. This being true, it is said to be your Original Face.[10] Heaven is not able to cover it. Earth is not able to support it. Fire is not able to burn it, nor is water able to dampen it. Even the wind is unable to penetrate it. There is nothing under heaven that is able to obstruct it.

Those for whom this is clear are feared even by the Maras, but those for whom this is obscure are deceived even by the heretics. For the person who is clearly enlightened concerning his Original Face, there is nothing in the universe that obscures or obstructs his vision. Thus there is no means of enacting the supernatural power of the Maras. Because such a person sees through to the bottom of his own intentions, the Maras fear and avoid him; they hesitate to draw near. Conversely, the person who is obscure and lost concerning his Original Face accumulates any number of confused thoughts and delusions, which then adhere to him. Heretics are easily able to deceive and swindle such a person.

When two of equal skill at this meet at swords' point, there is no conclusion to the match. The meaning of this is that if two men who had both penetrated their Original Face were to meet, each unsheathed the Sword Taia, and they faced off, it would be impossible to bring matters to a conclusion. If one were to ask about this, it might be likened to the meeting of Shakyamuni and Kashyapa.

Shakyamuni's holding the flower and Kashyapa's subtle smile. At the gathering at Gridhrakuta Peak when Shakyamuni was about to die, he held up a single red lotus. He showed this to eighty thousand monks and every one of them remained silent. Only Kashyapa smiled. Knowing at that time that Kashyapa had been enlightened, Shakyamuni entrusted him with the Correct Doctrine, which does not rely on the written word and is specially transmitted without instruction, and affirmed on him the Buddha-seal.[11]

Since that time, the Correct Doctrine was transmitted in India in twenty-eight successions to Bodhidharma. In China it was passed on from Bodhidharma in six transmissions to reach the Sixth Patriarch, the Zen Master Ta Chien.[12]

As this Zen Master was incarnated a bodhisattva, from this time the Buddhist Law flourished in China, spreading its leaves and branches, quickly promulgating the Five Houses and Seven Sects, and finally being transmitted to the Japanese priests Daiō and Daitō, through the priest Nai Chih Hsü T'ang.[13] This has been unremittingly continued from teacher to disciple to the present day.

The doctrine of "holding the flower . . . the subtle smile"

is difficult to arrive at and is not easily unraveled by guesswork. One must drink in the breath of all the Buddhas while swallowing one's own voice.

Although there is really no way to express this principle, if pressed, one might summon up the example of taking water from one vessel and pouring it into another so that the waters become mixed and indistinguishable. This is the moment when the eyes of Shakyamuni and Kashyapa meet and become one. Relativity is no longer there.

Among all martial artists of every discipline, there is not one in one hundred thousand who has grasped the purport of "holding the flower . . . the subtle smile." Nevertheless, if one did have the most steadfast of intentions and truly wanted to understand, he would have to discipline himself for another thirty years. Erring in this would not simply be a matter of not mastering martial arts; he would enter hell like an arrow shot from a bow. This is truly a frightening thing.

Raising the one and understanding the other three means that as soon as one part is shown, the other three are immediately understood.

Distinguishing subtle differences in weight with the unaided eye. Distinguishing... with the unaided eye means the eye's function, or measurement by the eye.

Differences in weight are extremely subtle.[14] The man who is able to measure out any weight of gold and silver by eye and not err by the slightest amount is a clever and skillful person.

These are examples of ordinary cleverness signifies that such clever people are ordinary and their number is legion, and thus there is nothing special about them.

If anyone has mastered this, he will quickly cut you into

three pieces even before the one has been raised and the three understood. This pertains to the person who has been enlightened concerning the cause of the Buddha's appearance in the world. It is he who will quickly cut you into three parts before the one has been raised, the three understood, or before any indication whatsoever appears. Thus I suppose that, in meeting someone like this, there is nothing that could be done.

How much more so when you meet him face to face? A man who has gained such celerity and subtlety, when meeting another man face to face, will cut so easily that his opponent will never know that his head has fallen off.

> In the end, a man like this never exposes the tip of his sword. Its speed—even lightning cannot keep up with it. Its brevity—it is gone even before the quick wind of the storm. Not having such a tactic, if one, in the end, becomes entangled or confused, he will damage his own blade or injure his own hand, and will fall short of adroitness. One does not divine this by impressions or knowledge. There is no transmitting it by words or speech, no learning it by any doctrine. This is the law of the special transmission beyond instruction.

In the end, a man like this never exposes the tip of his sword means that a master never, from the very beginning, shows the tip of his sword.

Its speed—even lightning cannot keep up with it. Its brevity—it is gone even before the quick wind of the storm. As for the speed of technique, this means that even the lightning, which is gone just as you think you have seen it, cannot pass through this man's movements. As for its brevity, it disappears even faster than the fine grains of sand that are blown before the storm.

Not having such a tactic, if one, in the end, becomes entangled or confused . . . says that without such skill, if one becomes just a little attached to the raising of his sword or just a little attached to the application of his mind . . .

He will damage his own blade or injure his own hand, and will fall short of adroitness means that he will definitely break off the tip of his own sword, will cut his own hand, and is unlikely ever to be called skillful.

One does not divine this by impressions or knowledge. "Impressions or knowledge" refers to the knowledge and discrimination within the human heart. *Divine* means calculating and figuring things out. What this means is that no matter how much you try to figure or calculate by means of impressions or knowledge, it will not prove the least bit useful. Therefore, separate yourself from the discrimination of figuring things out.

There is no transmitting it by words or speech, no learning it by any doctrine. For the true martial artist, there is no way to pass this on by words. Moreover, there is no way to teach or learn through doctrine what kind of stance to take or where to strike.

This is the law of the special transmission beyond instruction. It cannot be transmitted with words, and no matter what method one may take, it cannot be taught. Therefore this is called the doctrine of "a special transmission beyond instruction." This is a doctrine outside the teachings of an instructor, a doctrine that particularly requires self-enlightenment and realization on one's own.

There is no established rule for manifesting this great ability. Orderly action, contrary action—even heaven does not determine this. So what is the nature of this thing? The ancients said, "When a house does not have a painting of a Pai Che, it is like having no ghosts at all." If a man has tempered himself and arrived at this principle, he will control everything under heaven with a single sword.

For those who study this, let them not be thoughtless.

There is no established rule for manifesting this great ability.[15] If the "great ability" of the law of this special transmission should manifest itself in front of you, it will do so freely, without the existence of any established rule. And yet it is called the "great ability" because it extends in all the ten directions and is missing from no place by even the tip of a rabbit's hair. An established rule is a law or regulation; there are no laws or regulations such as would mold things concerning the manifestation of this great ability.

Orderly action, contrary action—even heaven does not determine this.[16] The man who manifests this great ability, whether he would act in an orderly way or a contrary way, is free and without obstacles.

So what is the nature of this thing? indicates confronting someone and asking him what something is in fact.

The ancients said, "When a house does not have a painting of a Pai Che, it is like having no ghosts at all." This is an answer to the preceding question.

The Pai Che has a body like a cow's, a head like a man's, and is an animal like no other known. It eats dreams and misfortunes, and in China they draw a picture of it to put up at the house entrance or to hang on the inner pillars. In short, putting up an illustration of Pai Che is for the purpose of avoiding misfortune.

The person who had no ghosts in his house from the very beginning would not even think about making a picture of Pai Che and hanging it somewhere. This is to say that he who has gained the use of either the orderly or the contrary, since even heaven cannot determine what is in his mind, completely transcends pain and pleasure. He has misfortunes in neither body nor home. Because of this, his mind will not hanker after a picture of Pai Che, and his own world will be a thing of beauty.

If a man has tempered himself and arrived at this principle, he will control everything under heaven with a single sword. This means that if one disciplines himself in this way, exhaustively tempering this pure metal a thousand times over, and becomes instantly free like the quick unsheathing of a sword, he should be like the founder of the Han Dynasty, controlling all under heaven with a single sword.

For those who study this, let them not be thoughtless. Those who study the mysterious principle of this sword should not easily take on thoughtless notions, but should strive to heighten their own luster. In intently continuing their own efforts, they should not be negligent, not even for a moment.

Notes

The Mysterious Record of Immovable Wisdom

1. Fudō Myōō is, literally, "Immovable Enlightened King." (Skt Achala.) One of the Five Wisdom Deities, in Zen Buddhism he is considered to manifest the true nature of all living things.

2. Kannon, a bodhisattva, the Buddhist Goddess of Mercy. (Skt Avalokitesvara.) Originally depicted as male, in one of the three common forms of representation she has a thousand eyes and a thousand hands.

3. The text here gives the names of the twelve notes of the musical scale used in China and Japan. Going up the scale, they are: *ichikotsu, tangin, hyōjō, shōzetsu, shimomu, sojō, fushō, tsuku-seki, ban (dakei), banshiki, shinsen, kamimu.*

4. Bukkoku Kokushi: 1256–1316.

5. Saigyō (1118–90): A Shingon priest of the late Heian period famous for his wanderings and highly admired as a poet. Eguchi was located within the modern city of Osaka. Saigyō is said to have stopped there one evening and asked for lodging, prompting the above reply by the courtesan.

6. It should now be clear that *concentrate on* might be used in the text as an alternative to *put the mind. Concentrate*, however, narrows the sense of the author's phrase in the original. Both ideas should be kept in mind.

7. The *tanden*, a point three finger widths below the navel, is considered by some Taoists to be the proper residing place of the mind. It is very nearly the body's center of gravity and is referred to often in martial arts' literature.

8. *Seriousness*, also translated as *reverence*, for the Neo-Confucianists meant an internal attitude of attentiveness and composure applied to efforts in handling affairs. As a desired state of mind, it contains a certain sense of meditation as well.

The quotation is from *Mencius* (Bk 6, pt. 1, chapter 11): "Mencius said, 'Human-heartedness is man's mind. Righteousness is man's path. How sad that he abandons that path and does not rely on it; that he loses that mind and does not know to seek it. When a man has lost a cock or a dog, he knows to seek it, but having lost his [proper] mind, he does not know to seek it. The Way of Learning is nothing other than seeking the lost mind.' "

9. Jien (1155–1225), also widely known by the name Jichin, was a poet and monk of the Tendai sect.

10. A favorite phrase of the Chinese Neo-Confucianists to explain "seriousness."

11. Mugaku (1226–86): A Chinese priest of the Linchi (Rinzai) sect, invited to Japan by Hojo Tokimune in 1278. The above story refers to the invasion of the Southern Sung by the Mongols in 1275.

A *gatha* is a metrical hymn or chant, often found in the Buddhist sutras. The entire verse runs, "In all of heaven and earth, no place to stand up a single pole. / Happily I understand: Man is Emptiness, the Buddhist Law is Emptiness. / How wonderful is the three-foot sword of the Great Yuan. / With the speed of a flash of lightning, / Cut through the spring breeze."

12. Shao K'ang-chieh (1011–77) was a scholar of the Northern Sung Dynasty. Rather than "lose," the verb here might be translated, "let go of."

13. Chung-fêng (1263–1323): A Chinese Zen priest of the Yuan Dynasty.

14. From the *Pi Yen Lu*, a collection of Zen problems, sayings and stories of the patriarchs.

A monk asked Chao-chou, "Is a newborn child possessed of the six perceptions?" Chao-chou said, "Throw a ball into a swift current." The monk then asked T'ou-tze, "What does it mean, 'Throw a ball into a swift current?'" T'ou-tze said, "It never stops."

15. A poem at the end of the twelfth section of the *Ise Monogatari* (ninth century). The section runs:

A long time ago there was a man who stole a young woman from another man and, when they went off to Musashino, being considered a thief, he was hunted down by the governor of that province. He hid the woman in a thicket and fled. A traveller said, "There is a thief in this field," and a fire was to be set to smoke him out. In her distress, the woman cried, "Today, burn not the fields of Musashino. / Both spouse and I lie hidden / in the grasses of spring."

16. The quotation is based on the *Doctrine of the Mean* (chapter 1): "There is nothing as clearly seen as that which is hidden, nothing as apparent as that which is dimly seen. Therefore the gentleman is careful when alone."

17. *Ranbu*: A dance rendered between performances of Nō.

18. *Sarugaku*, literally "monkey music," is an ancient form of drama and is the predecessor to Nō.

The Clear Sound of Jewels

1. *Right-mindedness* is the term finally chosen to represent the Japanese *gi*, although it falls short of being an exact equivalent. Among alternatives considered, *righteousness* was rejected because, at one extreme at least, the Westerner self-satisfied in his own righteousness is apt to embark on the task of correcting others. *Probity* ("unimpeachable integrity") is closer and should be kept in mind. The emphasis lies in the individual's first setting himself right, through self-reflection, training and discipline. This does not automatically, or even eventually, lead to proselytism, and many, in fact, are the stories in Zen and the martial arts of would-be students going to great lengths to receive the instruction of the master. *See also* p. 54.

2. The principle in dying is to recognize why, and in what way, one should die.

3. Ch'eng Ying and Ch'u Chiu: Two dependents of the House of Chao Shu during the Spring and Autumn Period (770–403 B.C.). Knowing an evil minister was planning to massacre the entire Chao family, Ch'eng Ying and Ch'u Chiu conceived of a plan whereby Ch'u Chiu and his son, who resembled the heir of Chao, would feign an escape and be killed, and Ch'eng Ying would flee to the mountains with the true son. The plan succeeded, and much later the heir was able to overthrow the evil minister and continue the House of Chao. Ch'eng Ying then recited the incident at the grave of Ch'u Chiu and committed suicide.

4. Po I and Shu Ch'i: Two brothers who lived in the last days of the Yin Dynasty (1766–1122 B.C.). At the time King Wu of the Chou was about to kill the last emperor of the Yin, the brothers admonished him, saying that it is improper for a vassal to kill his king. This advice was ignored and King Wu went on

to establish the Chou Dynasty. The brothers, feeling it would be to their shame to eat the barley of the Chou, fled to Mount Shouyang, eating only bracken. In the end, they starved to death.

5. The Six Desires: the desires aroused by the six senses of sight, sound, smell, taste, touch and thought; or the six sensual attractions arising from color, shape, carriage, voice, soft skin and beautiful features.

6. From the Golden Light Sutra: "The Absolute Body of the Buddha is like Emptiness. The manifestation of form in response to the material world is like the moon in the midst of the water."

7. The Twelve Links in the Chain of Existence: ignorance, action, consciousness, name and form, the six sense organs, contact, sensation, desire, attachment, existence, birth, old age and death. Starting with ignorance, each causes the next in the chain, so if ignorance is eliminated, old age and death will not occur. This is also referred to as the Chain of Causation.

8. Li Po (Li T'ai Po, 701–62) was one of the great poets of T'ang period China. This paragraph is the introduction to his poem, "Banqueting in the Peach Garden on a Spring Night," and this sentence is from Chuang Tzu: "This life is like a dream; this death is like a current."

9. The sense of *thing* meant here is "phenomenon."

10. A proverb dating from the T'ang period.

11. Ippen Shōnin (1239–89): Founder of the Jōdo sect of Pure Land Buddhism.
   Hottō Kokushi (1207–98) was a monk of the Rinzai sect who travelled to Sung China in 1249.

12. *Namu Amida Butsu*, "Homage to the Buddha Amitabha," is the liturgical and meditative formula of faith of, particularly, the Pure Land Buddhists.

13. Kogaku Oshō (1465–1548): A Rinzai monk who taught Zen to the Emperor Go-Nara.

14. The Ten Essential Qualities can, in accordance with the Lotus Sutra, also be translated as "thus" or "so," in other words, the "suchness" of a thing.

15. The Ten Worlds can also be explained as states or unchanging aspects common to all life. Some have alternate designations, as follows:

Hunger: Hungry Ghost (Skt Preta). They are in differing degrees of suffering and torment.

Anger: Demon (Skt Ashura). Lowly beings who in Hindu mythology were continually at war with the god Indra.

Heaven: Realm of the Devas. A place where the meritorious enjoy the rewards of good karma but do not make progress towards bodhisattva enlightenment.

(Man of) Learning: Hearer (Skt Sravaka). Originally a disciple who had listened in person to the Buddha's teaching; by extension in Hinayana Buddhism, any disciple of the Buddha.

(Man of) Realization: (Skt Pratyeka-buddha). One who lives apart from others and independently attains awareness of the Chain of Causation. (*See* Note 7 above.) He is in contrast to the bodhisattva, who chooses to stay on in the cycle of reincarnation to help others, as well as himself, attain enlightenment. Like a Sravaka, a bodhisattva may be either layman or cleric.

16. The lower six remaining in the world of illusion, the upper four achieving some stage of enlightenment.

17. Skt Avatamasaka. Japanese: Kegon Kyo.

18. Buddhahood (*Bukka* 仏果), *lit.* the "effect" (fruit) of the Buddha. Besides being homonyms, the characters for *ka* (果, effect) and *ka* (菓, fruit) resemble each other, providing opportunities in the following pages for some untranslatable punning.

19. In northeastern Japan there was once the custom of setting up a branch of honeysuckle at the entrance of the house of one's intended. If she agreed to meet, she would take it inside. If not, the suitor would put up another and another until there were said to be a thousand.

20. Mountainous locations in China.

21. The Five Roots are the five sense organs: the eyes, ears, nose, tongue and body. (*Cf.* Note 5 above.)

22. Consciousness (Skt vijnana). The sixth of the six means of perception (sight, hearing, smell, taste, touch and consciousness), it is mind in the widest sense of all mental powers, but especially the faculty of thought.

23. *Fan-i Ming-i Chi*: a Sung Dynasty Sanskrit-Chinese dictionary in seven chapters.

Annals of the Sword Taia

1. The fully indented paragraphs were composed in a terse Chinese style and are the heart of *Taiaki*. The longer sections in between, written in Japanese, are basically exegeses of the Chinese sections.

2. *Personal view* is a Buddhist term signifying an individual view based on the *erroneous* idea that the ego, or personal self, is reality and can perceive things realistically.

3. World Honored One is one of the ten titles of Shakyamuni, the historical Buddha. The Snowy Mountains are the Himalayas.

4. It is said that when Shakyamuni was born he took seven steps in each of the four directions, pointed his right hand to the heavens, and intoned this phrase.

5. This Buddhist term indicates situations in which one inspires respect by his deportment. The four are representative of all the states in man, which are calculated to number eighty thousand.

6. "Created phenomena" result from the law of Karma; "uncreated" are independent of action, word or will.

7. Mara is a Demon, the Sanskrit literally meaning "Robber of Life." The reference here is to the Deva Mara, who from his position in the Sixth Heaven obstructs the practice of Buddhism.

8. Kashyapa (Mahakashyapa), foremost in ascetic practices of the ten chief disciples, became the leader of the disciples after the Buddha's death.

9. The text here is unclear. Grammatically, it would seem to equate the example of the "one and the three" with the reference to Shakyamuni and Kashyapa, but this fits neither in terms of the total meaning nor with the development of the text.

The reference to "the one and the three" is probably from the Confucian *Analects* (7:8): "The Master said, 'I do not enlighten those who are not enthusiastic or educate those who are not anxious to learn. I do not repeat myself to those who, when I raise one corner, do not return having raised the other three."

The latter part of the sentence is from *Pi Yen Lu*, a collection of Zen problems, sayings and stories of the patriarchs. "Raising the one and understanding the other three, distinguishing subtle differences in weight with the unaided eye—these are the ordinary tea and rice of the Buddhist monk."

10. Original Face is the pristine nature of the Mind, as yet unstained by human affairs or intentions.

11. Not relying on the written word and transmission without instruction are two points especially stressed in Zen. They underscore the principle that one is to look into his own nature rather than rely on texts or the teachings of others.

12. Bodhidharma: The first patriarch of Ch'an (Zen) Buddhism in China, he is said to have arrived in that country from India in either A.D. 470 or 520.
   Ta Chien (637–713): Commonly known as Hui Neng, he was a pivotal figure in the development of Zen.

13. "Five Houses and Seven Sects" are the various sects and subsects of Zen.
   Daiō Kokushi (1234–1308): A monk of the Rinzai sect who studied Buddhism in China.
   Daitō Kokushi (1282–1337): A follower of Daiō Kokushi who is regarded to be the founder of Zen at Daitokuji.
   Nai Chi Hsü T'ang (1185–1269): Also known as Hsü T'ang Chih Yü, he was a Chinese monk of Linchi Buddhism.

14. The original text here defines the Edo period measurements used as examples.

15. From the *Pi Yen Lu*: "There is no set way for manifesting this great ability."

16. From the *Cheng Tao Ko* and possibly the *Hsin Hsin Ming*, two early treatises on Zen. The sources say, respectively: "Contrary action, orderly action—even heaven does not determine this," and "If you want to obtain its manifestation, do not think of order or contrariness."

Bibliography

PRIMARY SOURCES

Ikeda, Satoshi, ed. *Fudōchishinmyōroku*. Tokyo: Tokuma Shoten, 1940.

Ishikawa, Shiratsuru, ed. *Nihon no Zen Goroku, Vol. 13*. Tokyo: Kodansha, 1978.

SECONDARY SOURCES

Daihyakka Jiten, Vol. 16. Tokyo: Heibonsha, 1933.

Dai Nihon Hyakka Jiten, Vol. 11. Tokyo: Shogakukan, 1969.

Kato, Shuichi. *A History of Japanese Literature, Vol. 2*. Tokyo: Kodansha International Ltd., 1983.

Sansom, G. B. *A History of Japan, 1615–1867*. Stanford: Stanford University Press, 1963.

Sansom, G. B. *Japan: A Short Cultural History*. New York: Appleton-Century-Crofts, Inc., 1943.

Smith, Bradley. *Japan: A History in Art*. Garden City: Doubleday and Company, Inc., 1964.

Suzuki, Daisetz. *Zen and Japanese Culture*. Princeton: Princeton University Press, 1959.

Wilson, William S., ed. *Ideals of the Samurai*. Burbank: Ohara Publications, Inc., 1982.